Authentic You

Women Win@Work - Lead and succeed as the best you

Ishreen Bradley

First published in Great Britain by Bizas Coaching & Consulting Ltd

Copyright © Ishreen Bradley, 2016

The moral rights of the author have been asserted.

ISBN: 9781537260679

All rights reserved. This book or any portion thereof may not be reproduced without the express permission of the author.

For more information see
www.authenticyoubook.com

*"Based on research and experience, this book moves from summarising the problems and challenges faced by women AT WORK to **offering a flexible framework to create solutions and progress - for** women to lead and succeed as the best they can be. An essential resource for female leaders to reach their full potential."*
Cosette Reczek, Group Head of Organisation Design at HSBC

"Ishreen's reflective inquiries, inner power exercises, strategy gems and top tips will give you great structure as you explore for yourself what you want from your career and enable you to make it happen".
Dr. Ines Wichert, Head of D&I Centre of Excellence, Smarter Workforce at IBM Europe

CONTENTS

Forward	xi
Chapter 1 Why Bother with Authentic You?	1

Part 1: The Case for Action — **15**

Chapter 2 Here's the Evidence	17
Chapter 3 The Underlying Factors	29
Chapter 4 You Are Better Than You Think You Are	48

Part 2: Let Authentic You Emerge — **57**

Chapter 5 Don't Wait for Others, Build Your Own Future	61
Chapter 6 A Plan for your Future	71
Chapter 7 Manage Your Profile: Your Promise and Proposition	123
Chapter 8 Manage Your Profile: Get Your Message Out There	137

Part III: How it might go   **153**

Chapter 9   155
   Here's How Some of My Clients Did It

Chapter 10   173
   What Made it Work for Them and
   How You Can Do the Same

Addenda   **177**

Addendum 1   178
   Your Inner Power Toolkit

Addendum 2   197
   Some Strategies Employed by
   Successful Female Leaders to
   Overcome Underlying Challenges

Addendum 3   200
   What You can do for Your Organisation

References   203

About the Author   206

Acknowledgements   208

*…for my inspiring, entrepreneurial grandmother
who showed me that it is possible for
a little girl to achieve the dreams
she didn't even know she had.*

Foreword

The benefits of a more diverse workforce are well supported: greater diversity of thinking, better decision making, more innovation, and better engagement of our increasingly diverse customer bases.

But diversity does not automatically yield benefits. We need to enable diverse talent to bring their different perspectives, life experiences and values to the table. Only if this authentic self can emerge, will benefits follow. Being authentic means that we can invest our energies on furthering the causes of our team or customers, rather than wasting energy on hiding who we are and being side tracked by conforming to traditional definitions of success. Without this enablement, diversity can lead to 'us and them' thinking and create fault lines in our organisations. Diverse organisations need leaders who understand the value of diverse thinking and who have learned how to bring everyone around the table into the conversation and into the decision making process.

But authenticity is not only a matter of being given the license by others to be who you are at work. Often, we have not worked out for ourselves what career goals are meaningful for us. Instead, we have internalised our parents' aspirations for us or followed traditional definitions of success. For women in particular, knowing what we truly want out of our careers is not always easy to separate from masculine organisational norms on the one hand, and societal expectations of women and mothers on the other.

Authentic You is a coach in a book. Ishreen's reflective inquiries, inner power exercises, strategy gems and top tips will give you great structure as you explore for yourself what you want from your career and enable you to make it happen. The book focuses on three core aspects: purpose, promise and proposition. This is not a 'fixing the women' book that tells you how to behave in order to succeed in a man's world. Far from it. It is a book that invites you, and then guides you, through a challenging yet supported journey of self-discovery to define your own career goals. It will help you to reaffirm your ambitions and strengths, help you to recognise the road blocks and ultimately get you closer to meeting your goals.

Based on insights from a dedicated research survey of over 1,000 women, 150 in-depth interviews and a series of thought-provoking case studies of female leaders, this book provides many facts and figures, practical tips and real life application. Ishreen's in-depth understanding of the authenticity, gained through personal experiences as a young woman in a male dominated industry and from working with female leaders for well over a decade, shines through on every page in this very inspiring book.

While written with women in mind, many of the exercises in Authentic You are equally applicable to men. As women's roles change both at work and at home, so will men's and as a result everyone will benefit. With broader definitions of success available to everyone, we will all have the opportunity to find our unique and authentic definition of success.

Dr. Ines Wichert
Head of D&I Centre of Excellence, Smarter Workforce at IBM Europe
Author of *Where Have All the Senior Women Gone? 9 Critical Job Assignments for Women Leaders.*

Chapter 1 – Why Bother with *Authentic You*?

Over the last 25 years I have watched the efforts made by government and employers to develop the female talent pipeline. Whilst there has been a lot of rhetoric and some good progress in women reaching board level (mostly as non-executives) during that time, the majority of women at senior levels are not realising their full potential or aspirations at work.

With this in mind - and my experience of coaching a number of female executives to increased levels of success, I thought it was time to research the challenges facing female leaders at work.

My objective was to look at the question of the female talent pipeline from a slightly different perspective than government and employers.

I was interested in how women can do it for themselves without having to depend on external agents.

This book represents my thoughts and findings based on a 12-month research programme with survey inputs from over 1000 women in positions ranging from Senior Manager to C-level executive. It builds on the experience of successful female leaders – their strengths, the challenges they had to overcome and how they did it.

Its purpose is to be a useful resource for you to achieve the future you want for yourself by showing up as your best self – in a way that the value you have to contribute is obvious to everyone that needs to know. You will have the opportunity to look at how the underlying factors that typically get in the way may apply to you, find some ideas for achieving what's next for you and deepen your understanding of who you are by reviewing your authentic purpose and value proposition. This inquiry will enable you to plan your future and manage your profile by creating and communicating your promise and proposition in a way that is consistent with your values and way of working.

So when I speak here of *Authentic You*, I mean that you can stop trying to fix or change anything about you. I am calling for *Authentic You* to show up. For many of you, the people in your environment will not have seen that person. For them, you will be showing up for the first time as *Authentic You*.

This matters massively to me.

At the turn of this millennium, I was in a senior position at a big five consulting firm, pondering on a few fundamental questions:

- What is my true purpose at work?
- What is important to me?
- What contribution do I want to make at work?

These questions took me on an exploratory journey – looking at who I am as a human being and as a businessperson. On that journey I worked with an extraordinary coach to explore my values and engage with my purpose.

That was over 12 years ago. Since then, I have continued from time to time to review my purpose – each time embedding the learning so that I move forward in a way that is consistent with my values: distinctness, connectedness, finesse, insight, performance and courage. My authentic purpose at work is that each human being I work with gets to experience outstanding success and perform at their best in a way that is consistent with their values and purpose.

My life and my work now look nothing like they did back then. I discovered a passion for being with people when they discover what is really important to them - supporting them in developing and implementing new strategies for fulfilling their authentic purpose at work, performing at their best and producing out-standing results.

Working with female leaders in innovation driven organisations to reach their highest potential, be inspired by who they are and be fulfilled by their work is my life fuel. It takes me back to my roots and reminds me who I am.

In the last 12 years I have worked with many clients who have achieved outstanding performance and authentic fulfilment at work. I believe that you can too. Reading this book is your next step.

MY STORY

For the last 25 years, I have worked with hundreds of female leaders in many different sectors. Whether I was leading teams around the world delivering a strategy project, training people on improving their personal impact, or coaching them to let go of their doubts and fears so that they could go for that next big leap – a promotion, turning around a strategic and challenging situation or delivering a business critical initiative, my intention was and remains always to support them in their own growth as powerful leaders.

Having studied at an all-girls school in North West London, I grew up believing that it was completely normal for girls to excel in science and maths. I was therefore somewhat surprised to arrive for my course in the big smoke to find only 2 other girls in my engineering degree course of 100 people. That was my first experience of being around men in an educational or professional environment.

My first day in employment was at BT. It was definitely an interesting experience. Picture this scene: a 21-year-old woman – dressed in a navy blue tailored suit who thinks she looks absolutely professional - very excited and a bit nervous. As I walk with my manager through the room where I will be working and am shown to my desk, I notice each male in the room turn around and stare at me. Well – there was only one other woman in the room (our team secretary) and over 20 men – all engineers.

My manager gave me my first assignment. Going by his tone and expression, my impression was that he was not expecting much from me. In that moment, I decided that I was going to show him that I could do a great job...even if I did not fully understand at the time exactly what he was asking me to do. Well true to my word, I did a great job and everyone started to take note of me as a professional engineer.

After a while, I got very curious about how different people in the team behaved. Some of them progressed well and others just seemed to get the worst projects and assignments AND IT WAS CONSISTENT. What was that all about? I soon discovered that the people who did well were those who knew how to get on with people, had a positive attitude and took on challenges. This got me very interested in what makes people perform and I moved from being an engineer to leading the Quality and Training team for my Division of 140 people. My team consisted of two men and one woman – all in their fifties. I am not sure quite how they related to me, but I am sure that one of them felt that I had taken the promotion that they should have had - and that I did not know enough to be doing the job. This was very challenging for an ambitious 23-year-old. At the time, I was pretty much stereo-typed as an 'alpha female' and I heard more than one whisper that I had not got the position through 'kosher' means. However, my determination to do a good job (and show that I could) enabled me to lead the team to success and we produced previously unprecedented results – powerfully enabled by my thoughtful Secretary and my supportive group manager.

My effectiveness in this role – streamlining the training function, reducing costs and increasing adoption of training and development programmes, combined with enabling our Division to be one of the first to achieve the quality standards: BS5750 and EN45001 within one year resulted in BT sponsoring my MBA at London Business School.

London Business School was my first transformational experience. I went from being a logic based, process oriented engineer who thought in terms of project delivery to being inspired by sales, marketing and strategy. A whole new world was opening up for me.

As it happened, luck was on my side… although I do believe that we make our own luck in this world. BT was investing in a Video on Demand pilot and there was an opening for me to be the media sector marketing manager for our R&D Division – promoting all the sexy stuff we were creating in the labs out to our sales and marketing colleagues and end user clients in broadcast, print, publishing and advertising. My creative juices really got to thrive. I was able to showcase some of what was the most leading edge technology at the time and work with the sales teams to explore joint ventures with content providers as well as leverage our R&D brand to support BT sales to this sector. Life did not get much better than this!

Then I got pregnant. I was 29 and really conscious that age was not on my side, so very happy and excited that I was going to be a Mum.

Salah arrived on this planet in September 1994 and my world went from being about what I could achieve to how I could protect this precious new person that I held in my hands. I had to make sure he was looked after and that would take money. As the main breadwinner in our family, I knew that I could not give my son everything he needed and at the same time stay where I was at work. Our combined salary was just not enough.

I was being headhunted by a small hi-tech media company whose MD wanted me to help set up their marketing and consulting functions. The work sounded exciting and the MD was generous enough to let me work from home for a few days a week. They were also offering me nearly twice my salary. Probably not my wisest move to switch from a safe stable company and a job I knew I was brilliant at to a very small company in which I was the second most senior person – hence the second last to get paid. My hormones were all over the place and I found myself in tears because of the way the MD spoke to me. I was struggling to understand the business model, the technology and what she really wanted to accomplish.

The determination to succeed that had been planted in me on my first day at work in BT pulled me through and I engaged innovative new clients who invested with us to deliver some of the first client-server systems in the UK.

With this track record, I found myself being head hunted by a big five consulting firm. They were looking to establish a stand-alone media business unit and they found my track record, my experience and my contact list quite attractive. This was a fun and challenging time. We had next to no budget. I knew we had to be at the NAB conference in Vegas if we were to have any credibility and we were given £5000 to spend on this marketing push. Well it nearly covered the cost of hotels and accommodation! I found some free booths at the Las Vegas Convention Centre and booked in meetings with our prospective clients. It was a thrilling experience for me as I had also been invited to present a paper on what we were doing in Europe regarding the emerging multi-media application space. Looking back, what we were doing seems so trivial compared to what technology can do today, but this was way back in 1996. I had my picture taken with the centurions outside Caesar's Palace and some good press coverage was generated for my company. One of the contacts we developed was a key technology buyer at a national television broadcaster and this resulted in our winning a large contract for their new interactive TV joint venture with a telecommunications company, a high-tech set top box provider and a bank. This new joint venture was staffed by people from the parent companies – 4 completely different cultures and 4 very different agendas. My team and I supported them in creating shared values and a purpose for the leadership team, designing operating processes and resourcing requirements. My colleagues were busy sorting out the technology and hosting systems. A real accomplishment for us. We created a £12 million stand-alone business unit within one year.

My 7 years at this consulting firm enabled me to work with inspiring and talented colleagues around the world… on strategy, supply chain, customer relationship management and technology projects… most of which were transformational for our clients.

It was not all plain sailing however. As a single Mum it broke my heart every time I had to leave my little boy with family when I had to travel on work. I worried a lot about how this was impacting him. With the sequence of recessions and the economic squeeze, it was difficult to pick my assignments in London as I had been able to do previously. I was often surprised by my male colleagues with their nuclear families who said that they too would like to be based in London because they had children at home as well. I took a position in marketing so that I could be office based. I was fortunate that this job gave me good access to the most senior people in the organisation and a very high profile. However, I was conscious that I was earning way more than my peers in the team – and that made me feel guilty. I wondered if they would resent me for that. This was all making being employed quite undesirable to me. I started to reflect on whether I wanted to stay on there.

Towards the end of my time at the consulting firm I reconnected with my fascination for what caused initiatives, projects and organisations to be successful. It was clear to me that it is the extent to which people were engaged that resulted in the return on investment being realised. I looked at what most of the management consultancies were doing to support human engagement and decided that there was more that could be done. I found a US based consultancy that was causing exactly the kind of transformation that inspired me. After sometime, they wanted me to establish their UK business – but to do that as an associate.

So here was my dilemma: by this time, I am a single mum with a 9-year-old son to look after. Do I leave my safe job, six-figure salary and pension, risk it all and start again with no guaranteed income?

The pull was too great. There was a mission here that was calling me. I left the consulting firm, set up Bizas Coaching & Consulting and was engaged by the boutique American consultancy that became my first client. They trained me to be a great transformational coach – in one to one interactions as well as large group interventions with over 200 people at a time. I set up a unique business for them in the UK. We worked with a number of multinational firms in the pharmaceutical, financial services, entertainment, IT and High Tech sectors where we caused some tangible transformations for the organisations and their staff.

Seven years later, I found myself having itchy feet again. I wanted to create my own products and do a certain kind of work that was not consistent with the mission of my main client – the American boutique consultancy. I handed that business over to one of my colleagues and moved on to build the Bizas brand.

Since then, I have had the privilege of working with some amazing clients, travelling the world and making a massive difference to people in organisations involved with logistics, information and media, financial services, technology, engineering and design.

My experience as a woman at work, a mother and a business owner make me passionate about how women can progress in the workplace and fulfil on their aspirations with finesse and ease whilst having a fulfilled and happy life.

As such, I established an on-going research programme in 2014 to explore the challenges that women face in organisations that use STEM (science, technology, engineering and maths) disciplines and how they as female leaders can contribute to their own success. I called this group the 'LIFTED' sectors (logistics, information and media, financial services, technology, engineering and design). LIFTED because it is time women in these sectors are LIFTED; and LIFTED because as women, we are generally more interested in applying what we have learned than focus on pure theory as the components of STEM imply.

I believe this background and history qualifies me to contribute to women at work. If you are a woman looking at how to make the most of your life at work, I trust that you will find this book a valuable resource.

From Engineer to Enabler
As I write this, I reflect on the transition I have made from being related to as the "alpha female" engineer in my mid-twenties to being known as a supportive but challenging executive coach that

works with her clients to free them to be their authentic selves.

Why and How I made the shift
So why and how did I make this shift? Well the strategically minded woman who calculated what it would take to be successful in her mid-twenties started to work with an Executive Coach in her early 30s – believing that would bring her further success. Her coach asked her to do some interesting exercises that totally threw her. I remember being asked to draw a map of my communities. I really struggled with that and what I eventually produced illustrated how I had built a protective shield around me – with my close family, friends and colleagues separating and keeping me safe from the outside world. It was safe, but not a very inspiring life. As I said at the beginning of this book, I then started to connect with myself and what was really important to me. I did not expect working with my coach to lead to my getting divorced from my husband, or leaving my safe job. The upside was that my authentic female self-started to show through rather than the steel suited, detached heroine with all the external signs of success that I had created for myself. I was able to develop empathy and connectedness with my fellow human beings and feel very happy about who I am and what I contribute to the world.

So why else does this matter to me?
Our planetary ecosystem is starting to self-destruct; fabricated wars are causing thousands of human beings to be killed whilst greed is destroying neighbourhoods and human spirits.

I believe it is time for us women to step up and take responsibility for re-balancing the world and creating a sustainable future.

For too long we have taken a back seat. Now it is time to be equal partners.

It is time for us to co-steer our environment and our human race forward to a more fruitful and fulfilling future for our yet to be born generations.

This is why I invested time and money over a 12-month period to research and really understand the state of women at work and how we can move ourselves to an equal footing.

The Research Project
I mentioned my 12-month research project earlier, and I would like to share here my motivation and objectives of that work. As I am sure you are aware, the focus on enabling women to break through the glass ceiling and achieve their full potential at work has gained significant momentum over the last 3 decades.

Much of the existing research and recommendations ensuing from most research programmes focus on what Governments and Employers should do to improve the environment and enable women to progress. Yet, despite the efforts of both Government and Employers to address the challenges faced by women in the workplace, it could be argued that very little has changed in the last 30 years.

I am interested in the third leg that is holding this stool in place: the women who all this support is targeted at. So my question to you is: what can we as individuals and a collective do so that each woman fulfils on her aspiration at work?

This curiosity formed the following hypothesis for my research: *'There is something else at play that's impacting progress. Something that relates to women's behavioural and attitudinal response to their environment. By applying their strengths to these challenges, women can reach a balance/level that fulfils their aspirations, while supporting the continuing external initiatives designed to enable their progress.'*

The results of our survey of 1,030 women reveal that they possess the essential qualities needed to overcome many of the challenges that have traditionally kept them from progressing.

I interviewed a smaller sample of 152 female leaders for a more detailed one-to-one inquiry so that I could identify the underlying causes of these challenges and discover ways in which they had been successfully overcome

This smaller sample of 152 respondents was selected from sectors whose core business is based on STEM skills (science, technology, engineering and mathematics), and included women working in logistics, information and media, finance, technology, engineering and design (the LIFTED sectors).

These sectors have been identified by the Royal Society as key beneficiaries of STEM skills and key contributors to future economic growth.

How to navigate this book:
In the first part of this book I talk you through the research findings and underlying factors (Chapters 2 and 3), and show you how you are actually better than you currently think you are – no matter whether you are presently working at C-Level or as a senior manager (Chapter 4). The second part looks at how you can let *Authentic You* show up. You will get crystal clear on who you are - your purpose, promise and proposition, evolve a plan for your future and find new techniques to manage your profile (Chapters 5 to 8). Finally, I share with you how some of my clients achieved their aspirations and what made it work for them (Chapters 9 and 10).

Many of you will have the opportunity to impact a wider group of women through your organisations, so the third addendum provides possible ways in which you can actively engage your organisations in initiatives that make a noticeable difference for impacting the female talent pipeline. Please use it where you can to cause a meta-shift in what is possible. The first addendum provides you with a 'Power Toolkit' – and overview of some of the tools I refer to in the book and the second addendum summaries some strategies that successful women have adopted to dealt with the underlying challenges at work and realise success.

My intention in writing this book is that you as a woman with all the gifts you have available to contribute to the world have new insights that enable you to be your authentic self and fulfil on what is most important to you. I hope you find it of value.

Part I

The Case for Action

Chapter 2 – Here's the Evidence

In this chapter I lay out the findings from our research – looking at the challenges women face at work and the strengths they contribute. It makes for interesting reading. Take a look and see what is true for you and what does not match your experience.

As you read it, be aware that:

1. Not all the data is included here. It has all been validated by a statistician, but putting it all in here would make for a very dull read.
2. The quotes and data are presented as they were received. They are a record of what people said. In these two chapters I am not challenging, questioning nor defending what has been said.
3. You may find yourself strongly agreeing or strongly disagreeing with the data. Be sure to note down where that is happening for you. It will come in handy later on.

Challenges Women Face at Work
Fig 1. illustrates the top 10 challenges faced by the entire sample of 1030 women from senior manager to C-Level executive. It shows the percentage of respondents who identified the competency or behaviour as an area for development.

Over 50% of women identified managing profile as a key challenge, closely followed by personal/career development. In addition, the research found that the majority of competencies identified for development are related to visibility and impact (50% of the top 10 areas).

The following comment, made in response to the question: "what do you see are the key areas to develop yourself in going forward?" represents a common theme that women generally prioritise effective use of resources and time for the job in hand over actions that would increase their profile.

> *"I made good progress in the early part of my career by doing a good job...there comes a point where you have to do more than that. Managing profile – the thing I struggle with a little bit is that I don't see the point of going to more meetings if I don't think I will add value there. So I am happy to delegate to people who have the right knowledge and not duplicate. That does then mean that I don't necessarily get face time with a broad range of key business people in the organisation as I could."*

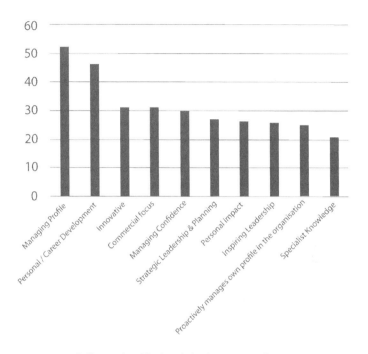

Fig 1. Top 10 challenges faced by female leaders in research project.

Whilst this behaviour is of benefit to the organisation as a whole, the interviews revealed that it inhibits women's progress.

In the current behavioural culture of most organisations, doing a good job in itself is not sufficient, one has to make sure that results delivered are recognised by the right decision makers.

Another respondent, had recently been made redundant and was looking for a 'C' level position at the time we spoke. Her comment indicates how a reluctance to invest in personal networks had an impact on her career and her ability to access other people to support her current aspirations:

"I was employed for 27 years and had the opportunity to develop a strong network but did not do that."

More About Managing Profile

Managing profile was the most identified area for development (52%). In the one-to-one interviews, women spoke of a number of factors that limited their capacity to manage their profile, including:

- Preferring to have results speak for themselves
- Being reluctant to self-promote although they know it's required to reach the next level
- Time: One respondent felt she would need to commit 20-30% of her time to managing her profile in order to progress
- A lack of confidence to speak up
- A lack of opportunity to build relationships with key stakeholders due to geographic separation
- A concern for credibility

The concern for credibility, can be summed up by the following statement found in one of the survey responses:

"I could be much better at letting others know what I have achieved i.e. actively seeking recognition. My own mind-set is that what I deliver is not as worthwhile as others."

Not managing profile effectively has certain consequences as summed up by the following respondent comment:

"Can I influence upwards? Do I have executive presence? I applied for a promotion but did not get it. The person who got it was more connected and social. My VP supported me and now I am concerned she will not support me in future, as I was not successful."

Personal Career Development

"It is very difficult for a female manager to get to top executive positions, as merit, productivity and people skills are less and less taken into account as one climbs up the career ladder."

Personal career development was identified as the second highest-ranking development area (45.6%). In some cases, respondents didn't feel they had enough time to dedicate to developing their careers given the job they had to do and other life commitments.

For some, it had not even occurred as something to focus on until they responded to the survey.
On the whole, those who had achieved more senior positions had thought through their career. They had managed to balance their priorities in a guilt free way, with a clear plan for how they were going to achieve their aspirations.

"…thinking about my own career development, I have never made decisions based on my own career. With my previous roles I focused on the new challenge - doing something completely new and

developed myself that way. Now I am beginning to plan my career for the first time in my life.

I might try for promotion in an area I worked in before…one that I left previously because I thought I was wasting my time and not doing anything useful with my time, as it was too abstract and too political – not concrete work.

I will definitely need to spend much more time on my network. But networking is a weak point for me…. going to cocktails and networks is a waste of time. I don't like empty discourse. I like talking about real things. So I really need to change my approach."

"Senior women start dropping off at my level because they won't go to battle. If they don't get recognised or noticed, then it is a competition – and a lot of women like me don't like that."

These two quotes from one-to-one interviews lay out the key elements that get in the way of women developing their careers:

- Becoming fully immersed and interested in the job at hand and not paying sufficient attention to their long-term aspirations
- Having to do work that they don't consider useful or sufficiently concrete as a stepping-stone to their long-term aspirations
- Not investing in developing relationships focused on supporting their career
- Being unwilling to play the political game

Other reasons identified by respondents for not investing in personal career development include:

- Mobility. Not wanting to travel as is required by a number of senior positions
- Not wanting to spend too much time away from family
- Being overly focused on delivering results rather than the things that would benefit their career
- Lack of support from managers both male and female
- Not knowing 'how things work around here'. A reference to the invisible rules that women don't know but believe that men do.

The Impact of Age on Managing Profile and Career Progression

Whilst you might expect young executives to be most concerned about career progression, an interesting trend was uncovered during the interviews.

A number of respondents in their 50s identified career development as a major challenge. These respondents were mostly in the VP and SVP category. Comments from this age demographic include:

"Being recognised as relevant as I am now older than many of my (male) colleagues."

"Sometimes you feel your gender and age goes against you when it comes to opportunities, as well as acceptance as a leader."

"Being overlooked for being senior and female"

A number of respondents in the 40-50 age groups felt vulnerable in their current positions as well.

A key driver here appears to be the pace of change of technology (given its importance to many of today's organisations) blended with the technology awareness, lower salaries and high levels of ambition of incoming 20-30 year olds.

In one conversation, a senior manager in this age group, with over 20 years of service for her company, was thinking of requesting redundancy. She was mentoring some new graduates and found that they picked things up so quickly and were so clever, that she felt she had little to contribute.

After a 30-minute conversation, in which I explored that manager's strengths and personal goals that she was yet to achieve, she began to see how much she had to contribute in terms of the value of her wisdom, skills, loyalty and relationships across the business.

She began to re-think what she wanted and is considering staying on in her job to fulfil on her goals and continue to contribute value.

It has become clear through these kinds of conversations that women benefit from a reminder of their value and contribution to the business.

Such small acts of recognition can be the difference between a female manager continuing to be an asset for the organisation or choosing to go elsewhere.

Strengths Women Contribute at Work

"Motivating and inspiring others. Strong emotional intelligence. I am a top performer that delivers results. I care."

Of the top 10 areas identified as strengths, 6 fall under delivering results; I am known to deliver (99%); I am good at my job (97%); I get results (95%); I am a good manager (87%); I demonstrate resilience in the face of challenge (82%); and I make a difference to the organisation (79%).

The remainder (4), relate to emotional intelligence (EQ); I make a big difference to the team (95%); people respect me (87%); I motivate others to change (84%); and I stand with pride (78%).

The highest-ranking Visibility and Impact quality, 'Is Visible as a Leader beyond own area' (70%) was in 22nd position and the highest-ranking IQ/knowledge based ranking; Grasping Complexities (20%) was in 37th position.

It is interesting to note that none of the VP and Director level respondents rated managing profile and personal/career development as a strength when asked to select 3-5 strengths from a list of 17 competencies.

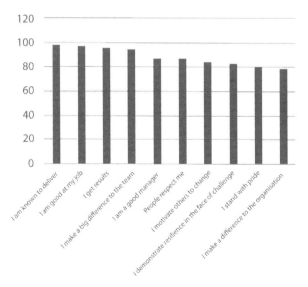

Fig 2. – Top 10 strengths identified by female leaders

When Delivering Results Becomes a Crutch
The following comments indicate the high level of importance respondents placed on being known to deliver, being good at their jobs and getting results:

> *"I am an excellent manager, able to motivate my staff so that they can give the best results to the organisation.*
>
> *"Very logical and results focused. Grasp complex issues quickly and motivate teams to work on solutions."*
>
> *"(I am good at) Understanding complexity and dependencies both. I could be much better at letting others know what I have achieved – technical and commercial and acting accordingly. Persistence in pursuing results. Flexible, happy with managing change."*

And the following comments illustrate a disdain for the political elements associated with being at work:

> *"The proverbial office politics. If it's not about results, customers, or employees, I give it no focus."*
>
> *"I prefer to have results speak for themselves."*

There is a general feeling amongst respondents that female leaders achieve progression by delivering results or having specialist knowledge. However, a conversation with an HR Director in an engineering company indicated that men progressing to similar levels have a more generalist background, implying that progression is not primarily dependent on results or specialist knowledge:

"There is a limited female leadership population. Women who have progressed have achieved this either by delivering results or having real technical specialism – so being overly consultative and overly deferential doesn't get you anywhere. Of the men at the same director level, some of them will be generalists."

Women use their Emotional Intelligence to Deliver Results – but NOT to Progress Their Careers.

The following comments supplement the respondents' qualitative scores:

"I work hard with energy and enthusiasm; I am able to grasp complexity when others don't seem to be able to. I then translate that complexity into something others understand."

"Energy and enthusiasm have got me success. This comes through when I love what I do.

"I have been told on a number of occasions that I am an inspiring leader. I am empathetic which means I can gain the trust of the teams I lead whilst maintaining the focus on the business goals we are pursuing."

"Building relationships, simplifying process and managing change and ambiguity"

"Building relationships with clients and a rapport to understand their business needs and frustrations"

From the interview logs it became clear that, although these are strengths women recognise in themselves and apply to their teams and work, a large percentage do not apply these same skills to benefit their careers.

Chapter 3: The Underlying Factors

Analysis of the data uncovered a number of underlying factors that could contribute to the thinness of the female talent pipeline further up the chain of command.

These include: confidence, an ultra-focus on results/doing a good job, guilt, organisational norms and expectations (time, mobility, conflict), lack of management support and 'The Old Boys Club'.

The term 'Old Boys Club' was much used by respondents both in the survey and in one-to-one conversations.

This section summarises findings for each of the underlying factors identified and possible implications for respondents in fulfilling their aspirations. Some strategies that successful women have used to effectively manage these underlying factors may be found in Addendum 3. How you can support your organisation in dealing with some of these underlying factors can be found in Addendum 1. The main body of this book focuses on showing the *Authentic You* in the eyes of yourself and others by sharing techniques with you for uncovering and communicating your authentic self and playing to your natural strengths.

Confidence

A lack of confidence was referred to by 47 of the 152 respondents in the smaller sample as a major challenge and area for development.

Confidence may be the one critical factor in the majority of men achieving their aspirations and the high number of women who don't. It is not limited to having an innate belief in one's own ability, which pulls to the need for external acknowledgment based on results produced. A lack of confidence may be triggered by many different stimuli that include: the pace of change – whether that is in organisational direction and goals, staff turnover and trusted colleagues leaving or as might be expected, the pace of technological change.

A fundamental source of low self-confidence seems to be when respondents experience 'being judged'. In contrast, confidence was high when they experienced 'being supported', as illustrated by the following comments from respondents:

> *"If I feel that I am supported in the venue where I am speaking, then I have a lot more confidence. If I feel like I am being judged or not listened to or I am going to get drilled – then you can tell it in my voice. I have presented information to my CIO on a subject area where I am very confident. If I think we are going into a contentious thing, then I am nervous about my ability to think in the moment."*

> *"I've always taken the next step but usually strongly encouraged by good management who are able to see my potential more than I do."*

"I've not really had to overcome barriers. Colleagues and managers have generally been supportive of my working part time or at home for childcare for example."

Some attribute their lack of confidence to a 'knowledge based' brain:

"I am very analytical and structured and so I tend to think a lot about what I am going to do – and sometimes I tend to think too much. I also have this problem talking about something that I don't know too much about. It's hard for me to fake confidence. But I see a lot of people getting away with it. They just have faith that they are going to figure it out later."

And yet others to the male dominated environment where they are confronted by being in the minority:

"…the other male leaders conspire against you. They see your execution capabilities and talk a lot about you. Managing their talk and keeping confident is tough."

A key source identified by a number of respondents was their own internal dialogue, which gets in the way of their progress:

"Confidence. I had to prove myself to my harshest critic – me"

"I talk myself out of being brave from time to time"

"Lack of confidence in my abilities. Feeling trapped by what I do."

"Not having the confidence that I could do the job."

"I think the main barrier I have encountered is visualising myself as a leader."

Many identified a focus on proving themselves to others by delivering results rather than representing themselves and their own aspirations powerfully:

"Personal confidence – I know I am a powerful person but spend so much time showing others I can support/deliver their agenda, that I do not build the profile and show confidence in my own agenda."

"Self-confidence has always been an issue, although this would not be visible to others. I would like to be better at disguising my emotions. I struggle to deal with people that aren't performing. 'Doesn't suffer fools gladly' is a phrase I often hear. To be more at ease in large groups when I don't know people – I find it difficult to mingle."

These comments point to self-doubt and a need for external acknowledgment of the respondents' ability.

Results Focus over Self-Promotion: 'Anti-Ego'

What's clear from the data is the respondents' belief that doing a good job and delivering results lead to both recognition and promotion.

Although those who have been most successful recognised that this changes with seniority, there seems to be a general reluctance to self-promote.

Many respondents felt that they should not have to self-promote. That doing a good job and exceeding expectations should result in their manager's sponsorship for promotion.

Some stated that men seemed to be good at self-promotion whereas women preferred to shine through their work.

There is also a tendency towards perfectionism:

"Perfectionism. I am improving here and accepting that 80% is good enough but I still have improvements to make here."

"Perfectionist – allow 80% to be good enough!"

"Delivering to the highest standards to both internal and external stakeholders"

Which seems to be driven by:

"fear of losing and fear of being laughed at, ultimately, as a woman all the eyes are on me."

In some cases, women feel they are 'not ready' if they have not reached a certain standard in knowledge and performance. It would seem that this level is on the whole higher for women than men, although the research used in this white paper has no specific data to prove this assertion.

Guilt

"Women can be their worst enemy, they give in to social pressure and their family. They prefer to live with guilt rather than make powerful choices."

Guilt was primarily associated with the need to balance priorities and the respondents feeling that they did not give sufficient time to the various commitments in their lives. Mainly their work and their families:

"I am not always taken seriously and feel guilty for taking time off to be at a sports day or kids play."

"Feeling patronised and made to work a lot harder to get my achievements recognised."

"Being judged – especially by other females outside of work as depriving my children."

"You were considered to be weak if you were authentic…so you covered yourself up. It cost relationships and a sense of numbness from having to cover up the guilt of for example, not spending time with your child."

Another area of guilt was a perception that the respondent had to manage their domestic partner's self-image:

"Being a threat to my partner and unconsciously being afraid of being powerful. This is something I have needed to work through."

Bullying/Derogatory and Defamatory Comments

Examples of both passive and active bullying were identified by respondents. In addition to being generally uncomfortable, the main impact was on the respondents' confidence and health.

One said that the 'poster-girl' pin ups that were found in the labs during the 80s have been replaced by more explicit, digital versions that were sometimes even included in internal team presentations.

Others related how they had experienced bullying on a scale that caused them to fall ill:

"I have had to overcome bullying in my previous company. No one intervened and stopped that happening despite good HR policies being in place. I internalised it, lost half a stone and fell ill. Then I had the risk of redundancy. I stood up to the bully, got a lawyer and won – but he did not apologise. Everyone pretended it did not happen."

"I put up with harassment for 18 years of my career as a woman and thought it was normal (as well as standing up for others). I got very ill as a result. Having to deal with a dominant bullying male boss really undermined my confidence."

On a more passive level, respondents report derogatory or defamatory comments, such as:

"Reluctance to take a female seriously."

"Bad language sometimes."

"Some of the 'in jokes' that go with male bonding"

And sometimes well intentioned or unconscious comments/behaviours that made respondents feel uneasy:

> *"Often being the only woman in a room full of self-confident ebullient men."*

> *"…people compliment my technical skills as being surprisingly good for a female, ask me to plan my career around my personal life or ask me why I don't have children"*

> *"When colleagues (male) feel the need to apologise for their behaviour (usually language) purely because I am female. If they need to apologise do it because their behaviour is unacceptable, not because they presume a woman would be insulted."*

Others spoke of situations in which men actively worked against women's progression:

> *"male prejudice to female execs becoming board members"*

> *"male leaders conspire against you. They see your execution capabilities and talk a lot about you. Managing their talk and keeping confident is tough."*

Organisational Norms and Expectations

Time

Whilst time was another major underlying factor for working mothers, it was also identified as a work/life balance issue for women who did not have children, as illustrated below:

"The need for a balance between time spent doing things I enjoy outside of work and time spent in/at work. Which is my choice."

"The pressure to always be visible. I am very firm about only being available when I am working. I keep my work mobile phone separate from my personal one. I TAKE holidays and do not connect. Despite this, the pressure to work long hours and deliver can take its toll. What makes me feel uncomfortable about moving further up the ladder is that I will have to make further compromise with my personal life (I already do an excessive amount of international travel) and I am not sure I am prepared to do that."

"Whilst I would like to achieve my next level (Director), I still want to maintain a degree of balance in terms of work/home life and I struggle to see the opportunity for this when I look at the hours worked by those above me and the expectations for this."

"Networking – both formal and informal – is still heavily drink and food based, taking place in pubs and restaurants after hours. This doesn't fit with my lifestyle and so I more often than not decline. It is hindering my career."

"Advancement in my industry seems to involve working fairly constantly – evenings, weekends, holidays."

A primary concern seems to be the organisations' and managers' focus on hours worked over productivity and quality of work:

"I have realised that being a manager in these conditions is getting tougher and tougher. So I am really wondering whether I will stay here in my current position where I have the seniority to become a Director and to get higher up than that because we are being asked for more and more work – not necessarily for more results – and for me, this is really a waste."

And for more senior leaders, the demands outside the core job:

"Time that others want from me being one of the most senior women in the UK. When do I do my day job?"

For working mothers and carers, the need to make efficient use of time and the desire to spend more time on activities and commitments outside work meant that less time was available for work.

As such, many 'optional' work related activities such as career development and managing profile gets sacrificed in order to deliver the work at hand and balance that with outside commitments.

"You need to have a nanny, cleaners and gardeners to be able to build a career unless your husband stays at home."

"I have to multitask a lot, as I have both a manager's job and a large family. This puts my schedule under

constant stress. I do not have the impression that my male colleagues bear the same pressure as I do."

"There is still a long hours culture and technology has led to an expectation that you are on call 24/7. To get on, the expectation is that you accept this. This isn't for me and I expect for many others either, irrespective of gender. Recognising that work life balance is an entitlement for all, not just women, people with caring responsibilities or those who don't want to move up the career ladder is key to this."

A number of respondents who are mothers said they moved to a less front-line role and took on flexible working/compressed hours to reach a balance that worked for them. However, they worry about other's perceptions of them based on these choices and feel a sense of guilt about the situation:

"Client facing roles are valued more, but it is difficult to do now as I have a young family.

"In my current role, which is non-client facing, I feel there is an element of "not a proper job" from some colleagues."

"As someone who is on a compressed hours contract I often feel I am being judged by some colleagues despite the fact I work more hours than some of my "full-time" colleagues."

"Having to say no to early morning/evening meetings and meetings on my non-working day (I work compressed hours – 33 hours over 4 days)

which means that everyone else has to work around me."

"Ability to work many hours and balance with family life. Only overcome by my partner changing his work patterns."

Mobility

The need to move location in order to progress or travel frequently for work were cited as barriers to taking more senior or higher profile positions. Respondents also cited the need to work across multiple time zones as a barrier.

In some cases, this was due to being the lead parent or carer. In others it was a life preference.

"My Family comes first with 2 young children and the fact I had to travel worldwide at short notice and for a long period of time were not compatible with my personal life – Consulting is a very fast-pace environment with no arrangement or flexibility given to mothers returning from maternity leave."

"I travel too frequently – I have refused jobs if it gets too much away from my family. I overworked so hard at one point with x kids on a highly stressful international job that I (fell ill) and took at least 2 years to recover." [edited to protect traceability]

"Networking – both formal and informal – is still heavily drink and food based, taking place in pubs and restaurants after hours. This doesn't fit with my lifestyle and so I more often than not decline. It is hindering my career."

"Lack of opportunity in my field of expertise. I will need to move into another area or leave the company in order to progress further because there are fewer job roles. I work in a global role and I notice that visibility is key. The challenge is to build a strong strategic network when you work remotely from the influencers and decision makers. Invariably the people that get the jobs are those people who get to meet each other and network face to face."

Politics/Unwritten Rules

Many respondents made reference to politics and the 'unwritten rules' of their work. This was true for some respondents despite having been in the same company for many years. For example:

"Understanding work paradigms/politics/ a woman in a man's workplace"

"The ruthlessness and nasty politics at some levels is off putting. It's a domain where being a psychopath is helpful. Nice people do not survive. It is a culture of bullying and blame."

"Lack of clarity / transparency on actual requirements for progression."

"Sex/gender barriers; paternalistic attitudes about women; lack of clear career rules"

Some have learned to deal with the situation by not giving it attention:

> *"The proverbial office politics. If it's not about results, customers, or employees, I give it no focus."*

Lack of Management and Executive Support

> *"There is still a tranche of the executives who don't walk the talk when it comes to messages around women and diversity in general. The small number of women who have made it to MD and Director level are treated differently than men of the same or lesser position."*

> *"Males are afforded higher salaries for the same position."*

Attitudes Towards Working Mothers

This appears to be a major external challenge faced by about 40% of respondents as measured by the number of respondents to the question: "what is the biggest challenge for your organisation in expanding the female talent pipeline?"

The following comments illustrate the impact on individuals and organisations of this challenge:

> *"I left my previous role as Finance Controller in my organisation because my promotion opportunities were limited. My managers assumed that as I had young children I would not consider working in a different location or having to commute so I was not put forward for roles. I left to become a management consultant and work away from home 4 days a week."*

"(in my last two positions) I had the opportunity to be in meetings with a lot of senior male colleagues where I was in a minority as a female. We had to discuss reorganisations, and I was sometimes really shocked about the perception of a woman.

Several times I thought a woman had the skills to be promoted but they were not. For example, one time I was told 'yeah…I'm not sure, she might be pregnant…you know she just got married and who knows.' The second time was a separated woman and they said 'oh I am not sure she can handle the pressure because she has her kids during the week.'

I really found this very disappointing because I saw them handling their own activity perfectly well. When I got separated myself, I just did not mention it to my client…just to be sure that he wouldn't doubt my ability to fulfil on my assignment. I found this very disappointing.

When I myself was at my last company, I got pregnant, the male colleagues would say 'now she got pregnant, she will go into a different life" and they didn't invest so much time with me."

"male dominated work place and also maternity leave after being at the top of my game and having to come back in and prove that I am still as dedicated and passionate as before I had children"

A Lack of Sponsorship

The need to develop relationships and sponsors to support career progression is seen as a challenge for a number of women. By contrast, they do not see the need to develop stakeholder relationships in order to deliver results and do a good job as an issue.

> *"Promotion now is about sponsorship rather than demonstrating execution of the job. The rules appear to keep changing and its dead man's shoes. Also depends on what assignment you are offered next and future roles in terms of visibility etc."*

> *"Promotion of those who are more friendly with Senior Manager above those who actually deliver"*

> *"Lack of career support from manager."*

Challenges with Managers

Respondents identified that certain challenges were exacerbated when dealing with female managers because of the sense of betrayal that goes with it.

The following quotes illustrate:

> *"In a world of male leaders and male subordinates, I am the thin layer of butter. Subordinates want to report to a man as they feel more important then. Superiors and peers want to give you un-important work. The superior also sees you as a threat."*

> *"...public criticism can be brutal – even women of women – you expect women to be friends and they can turn on you in front of all men or join the men, its funny (betrayal)"*

"Lack of understanding from other people (particularly women) on work-life balance and life outside the work place – Childcare topics are not worth talking about within the workplace."

"I feel judged by females as a working mum – this shocks me and I feel betrayed."

"In other tougher departments, it is more political. Especially the senior women – they are extremely tough. They don't care for people…for motivation. They are pushed and moved to more senior positions."

"Confidence was knocked when I didn't get a promotion because my (female) line manager said I am not strategic enough.

"I had to refuse a foreign assignment when I had my first child. I had to leave the company as it was perceived by my female manager as a lack of commitment."

"Women need to support women more!"

The Old Boys Club and Patriarchal Culture

There is a prevailing view that male networks in organisations are a significant impediment to women's progression:

"The fact I am female holds me back. There is an old boy network and I am treated as a child by some senior male figures."

"The good old boy network – people who have worked here for a very long time don't want to listen to outsiders with good ideas or valid industry-best practice knowledge."

"being left out of the 'boys group' amongst executives"

"Still an expectation that senior women have more to prove than equivalent male colleagues."

"Patriarchy's structures and rules have not been removed; just changed strategy. We, women are always treated as women, not as equals."

"The fact that I cannot integrate with males the way they do, so I am left out.

A number of more senior women, however, had managed to understand the rules of the club and in some case join them:

"I found out who is in the club, what the rules are and joined it"

An interesting story came my way when I was at an event in Westminster where Francis Maud was encouraging more women to take on non-executive roles in government related groups – what are popularly called quangos.

He related a story of an interview board that had rejected a woman he thought was ideal for the role they were recruiting into. When he asked the chair of the board why she was turned down, he was told that the woman asked the board why they thought she was a good fit for the role.

Francis Maud related how he was flabbergasted by this. That was exactly why (in his opinion) they should have given her the job – her willingness to explore the fit rather than sell them on why they should recruit her. Of course they mistakenly saw her behaviour as demonstrating a lack of confidence and self-belief rather than a mutual exploration of fit.

Chapter 4 - You Are Better Than You Think You Are

When I analysed the research and prepared the white paper, I was left with a sense of surprise and wonderment.

I had thought that the massive investment in the gender equality agenda over the last thirty years, and the increased general consciousness about the importance and the business case for having women at senior levels would have improved the situation for women. How is it then that women today seem angrier about the situation than I did back then? Their anger and frustration communicated clearly in the online survey – even before the individual conversations I had with them.

Granted that some things have improved – such as flexibility at work and increased maternity rights, but on the whole, attitudes from male (and some female) colleagues and the struggle to prove your worth seem to be as difficult as ever.

Perhaps the answer is not to look out to Government and Organisations to make it right for us. Perhaps we need to look within.

A number of women responding to our survey indicated that confidence is still an issue. You believe in your ability to do the job well – so you have good self-esteem. But do you believe in your actual value? What is your self-worth like?

In many cases, I find that women don't believe they are ready yet – or that they are not as good as they need to be to take the next step. They tend not to negotiate their pay as effectively as men – in fact, sometimes they just don't even negotiate or ask for a pay rise.

The truth that you have to confront is that you are actually much better than you think you are. It is now time for you to build your own future… own your greatness and go for it.

In this chapter you will look at how stereotypical female personas get in your way and how you can move beyond the constraints of those personas to fulfil on your aspirations.

Female Leader Personas and Common Constraints

We are all familiar with the negative stereotypes used about women. The most commonly heard is that of the 'alpha female' – the woman who is strong and dominant. The other persona does not have a frequently used term, but is described as meek and gentle – not standing up for her rights – caring more for other people than producing results and sometimes a bit of a victim – blaming others for their situation. For the purposes of this book, I will call this second persona 'fluffy'.

As you will see in this chapter, neither term is meant to be derogatory. They are used to explore the source of certain behaviours that impede you so that you are able to understand how you can start to own and use those characteristics in a way that benefits you.

You may recognise yourself as an extreme alpha, an off the scale fluffy, or most likely somewhere along that spectrum. There is no good or bad here. The purpose is to explore the extremes and find your position in the spectrum.

So how did this persona arise in you?

My favourite theorist on this subject is Alice Miller. Miller, in her book "The Drama of Being a Child" describes how parents project their feelings, ideas, and dreams upon their children. A child, wanting to survive and be loved, learns to obey. She represses her feelings and stifles attempts to be her authentic self. The consequence is that the child either falls into depression or loses her sense of self by developing strategies to gain parental attention.

'Grandiosity' is the term Miller uses to describe these certain behaviours that children learn in early childhood to access attention and love (primarily) from our mothers. After all, in early childhood, who else is there? Your life depends on and revolves around your mother.

The moment you feel a loss of the level of attention you crave, you develop ways of regaining that attention.

Some people turn to working hard and producing results; others become excellent at looking after people, caring for others, being funny, looking beautiful, acting, dancing or even becoming over weight.

If you are an 'alpha', you learn to work very hard and very fast. You excel in everything you undertake – you are admired and envied for your success. It develops a kind of arrogance in you about your ability to produce results. This arrogance can at times show up for others as abruptness or rudeness. You may have contempt for others who do not have your intellectual gifts or your ability to produce results. You are impatient that they take so long to understand and can't keep up with you. You are successful whenever you care to be, but for some of you, behind all this lurks a feeling of emptiness and self- alienation. These feelings will come to the fore as soon as the drug of grandiosity fails – as soon as you are not 'on top', not definitely the superstar; or whenever you suddenly get the feeling you have failed to live up to some ideal image or have not measured up to some standard. You may feel that without your achievements and gifts that you could never be loved. It is less painful to think that others do not understand because they are stupid – isn't it? In these moments you are plagued by anxiety or deep feelings of guilt, shame and being on your own.

If some of this sounds familiar to you, it is possible that you are what the stereotypes would call an 'alpha female'.

Next to the persona I am calling 'fluffy'. This persona is developed where a mother is needy and returns attention to you when you look after her needs. The child learns the behaviour of making sure the mother is alright in order to receive love and affection from her mother in return. As a 'fluffy' child, you develop the ability to perceive and respond intuitively and unconsciously to the needs of others. You get a sense that you are needed, and this need guarantees you a sense of existential security. However, you may become resentful when you see someone else getting the attention that you think you deserve – especially if you don't think they have earned it.

Miller posits that one can be free from this trap only when self-esteem is based on authenticity of one's own feelings and not the possession of certain qualities that bring you attention from others.

The grandiose person has an 'as-if' personality: revealing only what is expected of them and hiding the rest such that people don't get a sense of who they are. I have found the term 'imposter syndrome' widely used in popular coaching conversations when this behaviour is being discussed.

So the good news is that you can start to own these personas in yourself and apply them to the benefit of yourself and your organisation.

Let's explore the two extreme personas so that you can deepen your understanding of how they got created, what triggers them, how they are perceived and the impact of living with that particular persona.

The Alpha Female

The persona of the Alpha Female was created when you realised that producing results, working hard and driving a situation enables you to get the attention and acknowledgement you seek. This characteristic evolves from childhood but usually embeds itself as a strategy during the teenage years.

A woman who fits this stereotype will be seen as ambitious – sometimes at a cost to others. You drive yourself and your teams hard. You may put the result ahead of the individual's needs and hence be called a 'ball buster' or some such irreverent turn of phrase. From time to time this may cause you to feel lonely because deep down inside you don't want to be seen that way…you do care about others and want to be able to connect with people – if only you knew how.

What do you do when a persona you constructed way back in your childhood to ensure that you received love and attention is now having the opposite effect?

Remember that none of these characteristics are good or bad in themselves. In fact, it can be a set of qualities that are admired in most men. They enable you to deliver unprecedented results that are valuable to your organisation and make you feel good.

However, as a woman, you have to be aware of the unconscious bias you have to deal with when demonstrating these characteristics. Human beings in general believe that a certain type of behaviour is good in a man and others are good in a woman.

You may not agree with this broad stereotyping – neither do I. The fact is that it still goes on – less at a conscious and verbalised level nowadays, but these opinions are still there – lurking beneath.

You may already know that it does. Your fear of being judged negatively by such opinions has a massive impact on your self-expression. It causes you to shrink when fear overtakes you. It causes great sadness in moments of quiet reflection. You long to be able to form lasting, deep and intimate relationships with your co-workers – like you see others do. But how?

My best advice for dealing with the downside of this stereotype's behaviour is to not resist it… learn to accept and acknowledge the benefits to yourself on a regular basis. Appreciate who you are and what is good about you as well as the value you contribute. Once you feel a bit more comfortable with these characteristics – and need less to hide them, you might start to acknowledge the characteristics in you to others where appropriate and acknowledge that it does not always work. Maybe request support from people who appreciate who you are and what you provide at work.

One of the women I interviewed had a brilliant technique for dealing with prejudices against this persona.

She said that often, men relate to strong women in the way they related to their mothers or their strictest schoolteachers. So, as a strong woman, you are already starting on the back foot. To dilute the impact of this, she would go out of her way to be kind and generous to them and support them in difficult situations. Show her feminine and nurturing side. It can seem counter-cultural and will take some effort on your part, but it clearly can work, so you might want to start practising.

Owning 'fluffy'
The persona at the other end of the spectrum is often described as 'being too fluffy.' I am not sure I have fully understood the breadth of what people mean when they say this - other than you are more focused on the needs of people than on the task at hand.

You may get very upset seeing the way the 'alpha female' persona communicates with people. But you would rarely speak up against that kind of behaviour for fear of causing a scene or upsetting people. Later, you may speak with a colleague to get it off your chest.

When you are at your best, you use your emotional intelligence to diffuse situations. In other situations, you may have a tendency to manipulate.

Sometimes you are told that you need to be more assertive.

You sometimes get upset that your work is not being recognised. That others are being promoted over you.

Your team is loyal to you and will generally go the extra mile. But there are those that have a tendency to ignore you or not do what you have asked them to do.

You are sometimes sidelined in conversations because you don't speak up.

These traits may have been learned from observing elders/more senior people around you and knowing that you can be safe by staying quiet. Or, you may want to make sure everyone is ok because you had observed bullying or bad behaviour towards someone when you were younger and you decided that you would never, ever be like that.

Whatever the source of this behaviour, you must know that the most successful men and women at work apply this kind of emotional intelligence to bring out the best in their teams and in themselves. They also apply these skills to support their careers by developing mutually beneficial stakeholder relationships.

So my advice to you is rather than hide your light under a bushel, be proud and 'own fluffy.' When people tell you that you are 'fluffy' or any such similar term, ask them what they mean by that – what behaviours they see that are not useful. Remind them that these are the skills that are highly valued in the leaders of today. You have strong beliefs around fairness and justice and want to make sure the people around you are protected. Think about how you are going to use those skills to develop yourself and your team to produce great results for your company and to ensure that you and the people reporting to you are recognised and successful.

My Transformational Experience from Alpha through Fluffy to 'At Choice'

I share my own personal experience by way of supporting your exploration. You may recall from my story that I was definitely an alpha – hard working, impatient, results producing intellectual through my teenage years and early adulthood. However, as I look back, I see that I switched from fluffy to alpha and then back to fluffy before I was truly able to own and gain power from both characteristics.

As a young child, I felt a strong need to look after and protect my mother. I am not sure where this came from, but I have vivid memories of destroying a cockroach because my Mum was screaming with fear. I wanted to make her feel safe.

Once we arrived in the UK, I became more strategic and saw the benefit of producing results and being driven. The 'alpha female' characteristics stayed with me from the age of 16-35 – when I started working with a great coach.

Working with her, I learned to own and value both sides of my persona – through which I was able to find my authentic self and my purpose: each human being I work with gets to experience outstanding success and perform at their best in a way that is consistent with their values and purpose - starting with me. Being able to value my different personas has allowed me to just let them be – and sometimes even choose the one I am going to wear to produce the best outcome for myself and the people I am working with.

What I have learned is each persona is a facet of the authentic me.

Part II

Let Authentic You Emerge

Getting the best from this section

This is where the work gets done to uncover and present *Authentic You*. It is a rich and mind opening journey that connects you deeply with you.

This is a journey that many of my clients have taken with me, and here I share the journey with you. As your guide on this journey, I have replaced the luxury of in person conversations with four types of exercise.

REFLECTIVE INQUIRIES
INNER POWER EXERCISES
STRATEGY GEMS
TOP TIPS

You will also find guides to some of the tools I share with my clients in the POWER TOOLKIT addendum at the end of this book.

There are several ways in which you can choose to travel on this journey:
1. You can take the quick 'city tour' and stay on the bus to get the essence of the journey – leaving out the reflective inquiry and inner power exercises. If you do this, you will end the journey knowing the main landmarks, but not really having absorbed the essence of the journey. Your head will know what is required, but your heart and gut will not have engaged. The experience of the journey will fade over time. If you choose to travel this way, just read the book from cover to cover without stopping to delve into the inquiries and exercises.

2. You can take the 'step on – step off' tour where you take the tour sequentially and stop off at the places that are of interest to you – areas that you want to explore in more detail. This mode of travel fits in with a busy modern lifestyle and can work so long as the excursions you take are the ones that you have been avoiding so far. You can travel this way by only stopping to work on the inquiries and exercises that you want to explore further.
3. Or you can hire a guide to walk with you on the journey. A guide (coach or mentor) will ensure that you go to the places that you don't want to visit whilst making sure that you are safe and that you get value from the whole journey. You do not have to take the whole trip in one go because the guide will rest with you and make sure you keep going where you need to.

Some of you may try to do the whole trip quickly, intensely and in depth by yourself. This mode of transport I do not recommend. This journey is more of a luxury cruise around the world than a high speed boat race along the River Thames.

Whichever type of journey you choose, I invite you to look upon this journey as the best investment you could make in yourself and relish every moment.

Chapter 5 - Don't Wait for Others – Build Your Own Future

Many women miss out on fulfilling on their aspirations because they either wait for things to change in their favour – or for the right time to take action. The impact is that their internal dialogue runs the show, their confidence gets impacted, they make more sacrifices than their colleagues or domestic partners which then further impacts their self-worth and health. They begin to resent their colleagues – senior and junior, their partners, their environment and get into a negative, disempowering spiral. This vignette is exaggerated to make a point, but you get the idea.

Step 1: Accept that some things may never change

Whilst you may believe that they should – and it may even make sense that certain attitudes and circumstances change, you may find yourself waiting a very long time for progress unless you do.

A more useful approach for you may be to accept that certain things/people are just the way they are and choose to take charge of your future.

Now I am not saying that you should give up on your core beliefs, but just that it may serve you better not to expend a disproportionate amount of time and energy trying to change them – or worse still, waiting for them to change.

Here are a few common themes that I come across in my practice:

Anytime anywhere availability

It is a fact of life that technology has made it possible for you to be reached at any time of night or day. This combined with the global nature of most businesses means that the traditional 9-6 job is a thing of the past for most of you.

Some women get rattled by this and resent having to be available. What's the point?

If you choose to work in a global firm with such requirements, it would be more useful for you to accept that this is how it is when you are working to progress your career.

Make arrangements with friends or family to make sure you are supported – especially if you have small children who might suddenly run into the room and want a hug while you are on your 6am global call in the home office. A smarter way is for you to use this requirement for flexibility from your employer to buy yourself some flexibility when you want to take short leave – perhaps to attend your daughter's sports day or your son's concert.

Oh – and don't you let yourself feel guilty about that.

The benefit of the anytime anywhere availability model is that it does cut both ways. It is your job to make sure it cuts both ways equitably and not let yourself go down the guilt/embarrassment black hole.

By the way, this does not apply JUST to those who have children or carer responsibilities. Some of you may want flexibility to join an art class or train for a full marathon.

So that deals with anytime.

How about anywhere? There are two forms of anywhere: anywhere for work during the week and abroad for a longer stint that adds to your promotion credentials.

Well, if your company requires you to travel on work during the week and you have commitments at home, this can be tricky – particularly if you have children or carer duties. There are two questions to ask yourself:

Is this way of working consistent with my work and home aspirations for the future?

If yes, can I make this pattern sustainable over the short, medium and long term – and how?

If the answer to these conversations is 'no' then go straight to Chapter 6 and take a look at what is really important to you and what you want to accomplish in your life.

If it is 'yes' then work out how you will make it work.

Attitudes towards women returners

Many of the women I interviewed said they experienced being judged by people at work and in their social environment for being working mothers. Again, just know that human beings are judging machines. They don't know your circumstances and they are looking at what you are doing through their own lens.

Know that you have to make decisions for yourself based on the constraints, barriers and opportunities that you face as an individual or a family.

This can be difficult and challenging, but if you are to have a corporate career that will be something you have to take on anyway.

The key to breaking through this is to stand firm in your values and purpose and being authentic to who you are. More on this in Chapter 6.

Then there are those of you who have chosen a different role while your children are young. This is a very practical way of managing work and home objectives – reducing travel whilst still maintaining your career trajectory.

Women I interviewed in this space often felt undervalued at work. If this is the case for you, ask yourself whether this is true in reality or in your head. Either way, what does it buy you being disempowered by other people's perceptions? The core question to ask yourself is: "Am I being true to my values, purpose and life objectives?" If you are, then you need to find strategies for managing other's perceptions of you. More on this in Chapter 7.

Prevailing Styles – organisation culture and/or management styles

In many organisations, there are articulated and documented ways of working and then there is the reality – that much is encoded into the culture and behaviours – often unsaid. There are also informal networks and people who have a 'say' in how things work that may not be immediately obvious for you.

If you find yourself where you know how things 'should' work but they seem to be working in another way – that you don't quite understand, it is possible that there are cultural norms and ways of working that are embedded in the organisation that you have not yet learned.

The best way to learn these 'invisible rules' is to watch and listen for how things are working, identify the key influencers and develop a rapport and working relationships with them. More on this in Chapter 8 (Manage your Profile – Get Your Message Out There) where I cover a simple technique on stakeholder mapping.

The research identified many issues with patriarchy, gender discrimination and bullying – both by male and female up-lines. When it comes to these issues of different management styles, you could follow the written HR processes and formalise your complaint. As you will have read in Chapter 3, this is often the last resort and is often not the best way forward for your career.

My recommendation is that you use your emotional intelligence skills to approach the situation in a smarter way. You will need to reflect on the kind of person/people you are dealing with and create strategies for influencing and being assertive in such a way that you restore your own sense of agency and purpose. Some ideas that can support you may be found in Chapter 8.

Step 2: Stop worrying about what others think BUT start paying attention to it

This can be the most challenging element that may never change. It involves having constant conversations with yourself to silence your 'self-talk' about what others may think or say and accepting that people will always have their multitude of opinions – most of which conflict with each other. Your challenge is to manage that 'self-talk' that is designed to protect you from harm - but that can sometimes hold you back from owning your full potential and realising your success. You will then be able to pay attention to what is being said without getting caught up in disempowering thoughts and feelings and free yourself up to manage how you are perceived.

Step 3: Plan and act – don't just wait: impact of waiting for the right time

You may have noticed that many women wait for the right set of circumstances or until they have the perfect set of skills before they take action to pursue their goals. This applies whether it is a career aspiration such as a promotion…or a personal aspiration such as starting a family.

When it comes to promotions, a woman will often wait for just that one extra qualification before they can take on a more senior/commercial role…or another year or two's experience just to make sure they are fully ready. Sound familiar?

The problem with this if you keep waiting is that those who believe they can learn what they need to when they need it will leapfrog you. Most likely, if you fall into the 'waiters' category, you probably know more already than your colleagues who just go for it.

Then there are those women who wait to get to a sufficiently senior position before starting a family. They wait until they feel they are established. The problem with this – particularly if you are in a front line role – is that you become mission critical and your absence from work is noticeable to those that matter. Marie Melnyk, protégé and number 2 to Sir Ken Morrison (who I have had the pleasure of spending some time with and who was a senior business leader in a £multi-billion turnover company) believes that in some cases it is better for women to have their families early in their careers when energy and physical fitness are at their highest, so that they can choose powerfully what balance they want between family and career while they are still relatively under the radar. By doing this, if you choose to focus on your career, you can establish the support structures and create a foundation for career success early on and when you are relatively un-noticed in your organisation.

Marie goes on to say: "once on their career trajectory (usually in the 30s), women do need to really think through their life plan if they haven't already done so. Although there is legislation designed to protect women and a greater awareness of working mother's needs, the truth is we don't live in a perfect world. Business moves on ever quickly not least of all in today's hi-tech/digital age. I would encourage any working mum particularly those taking longer periods of maternity leave or a career break to devote to bringing up children, to build in some 'me-career time'. Keep connected, keep up to speed with your industry, brush up on skills especially IT or professional. It's hard enough getting back into the swing of the workplace when the time comes. It's even harder if you 'fall behind'. Do work on practical things that will help your confidence on returning to work."

One woman I interviewed as a part of the research actually chose to wait until her children were grown up before starting her career. She went to University in her late 40s and started a career that is now on a fast track.

The point here is to know that you have options and to plan early so that you can choose rather than be given by events that happen around you.

The consequences of waiting are many
First, you will be giving a voice to your internal dialogue. You know that little person who lives inside your head and says things like: 'you can't do that… you are not ready yet… not good enough… he is so much more experienced than you are… is it the right thing for you to do anyway? … you don't want to fail… no it is definitely wrong…definitely a bad idea'.

This will diminish your confidence and slow you down.

If you are in a relationship and you want to balance that with achieving your full potential at work, your choosing the slower career track will mean that you end up dealing with the emergencies and make more sacrifices than your partner. This will not only impact your sense of self-worth, but also possibly your health and cause you to resent your partner.

Of course, if your wish is to focus more on your relationship and you choose powerfully that your career comes second, that will work. You may from time to time need to remind yourself that you made a choice to put your career second to your partner's and then what there is to do is to support them in being as successful as they can while you ensure that your family is nurtured and fulfilled.

In case it is not clear yet, the message here is to avoid waiting and take action – preferably supported by a clear plan and goals.

Step 4: Let go of the guilt and fear that has held you back

In order to create a sustainable future that inspires you, you must learn to focus on your own greatness. Start a list of your successes in life in a format that inspires you. This could evolve into a drawing, a word picture, or a collage that you refer to for an instant lift. You may want to start with a basic list so that you can get going quickly.

Find and be your authentic self – not the default and automatic persona that you constructed through a script way back in the past to keep you safe – your alpha or fluffy persona, for example. You may want to reflect on where guilt has got in the way for you in the past, get to the source of it and let it go. One technique for doing this is exploring your script around the conversation about guilt. More on this in 'Keep it Alive', Chapter 6.

These aspects of uncovering *Authentic You* are easy to write, but take a long time to master. It is a journey of self-discovery that can be challenging and demanding on your current sense of who you are. As you develop yourself to know who you really are, you will find a sense of freedom and lightness that will enable you to propel yourself forward with velocity.

Presenting the authentic rather than the pretend you will automatically result in more connected and real conversations. You will develop trust-based relationships because people won't be put off by what they can "smell" as not being quite right.

Step 5: Make powerful choices

Often what holds women back is that they fail to make powerful choices to move forward. Moving forward is different for different people and is a function of many things, including age, life stage and personal ambition.

It is important from time to time to take a pause and reflect on where you are, where you have been and where you want to head.

When you do this, you absolutely must make sure that you are making choices and are willing to be responsible for those choices. For example, if you choose to take a back office role while your children are small, it is not helpful to let your internal dialogue make you worry about how you are perceived by your former colleagues – know that it is a choice you made for where you are now. Such choices are more digestible if you take them in the context of a wider life plan rather than focus on the circumstances you find yourself in 'now'. The next chapter covers some fundamental aspects that will enable you to make powerful choices and create an inspiring future for yourself.

Whatever situation you find yourself in, whatever choices you make, however good you are at what you do and in leading your teams, one thing you want to keep developing yourself in is to be conscious of and actively manage how the *Authentic You* is perceived by your colleagues and key stakeholders.

Chapter 6 – A Plan for your Future

Get in touch with your passion and purpose
Many women trundle through their careers and life in general without a clear view of what is really important to them. Finding clarity of your purpose, values, what you stand for in life, what is important to you and what lights you up, is critical to creating a vision for your future.

With this vision, you can start to look at where you want to focus your time and energy. It will enhance your experience of living a meaningful life and impact your sense of self-worth and value. You may find your passion and purpose lies mainly at work…at home, or (as with most people) a blend of the two that inspires you.

1. Create a solid foundation for *Authentic You* to emerge

A few tips for letting go of the guilt, fear and procrastination…the things that stop you in life.

Often people dive into creating an inspiring future without dealing with what gets in the way. This is like building your house on quicksand. Not recommended.

For me, it is essential to at least surface what gets in the way for you…whether that is your version of guilt, fear or something else. What makes you give up on what seemed like a good idea at the time? What makes you procrastinate? All things that stop you from having what you want in life.

My favourite technique for dealing with what stops us in life is 'script theory' as popularised in Eric Berne's book *'What Do You Say After You Say Hello?'* published back in 1972.

You can use this technique whenever you experience being upset or disempowered. It is very effective if you apply it in the moment. It can also be useful to sit down and reflect on what gets in the way for you.

Reflective Inquiry: A trip down memory lane – the dark side

Look back over the story of your life and identify situations that impacted you negatively. See if you can identify any extreme moments where you did not show up as you would wish – where the actions you took were not ones that you were proud of, and where the result and impact was not what you wanted - where you experienced being afraid or guilty.

Much of our subconscious time is spent in dialogue with these scripts – continually confirming, disconfirming, modifying or regenerating them – although they may be accurate or not in differing degrees. These dialogues are what I have referred to as your 'self-talk' in this book. They are the lenses we use to examine and understand ourselves and others.

The script sequence usually goes like this: something happens and you make a decision based on that occurrence. You then experience feelings associated with that decision. These feelings drive behaviours and actions that either deliver the desired outcome – or not. With this information, you then adapt your original decision – or keep it as it is. Sometimes these decisions empower you and sometimes not.

You may see clearly how the scripts you created and reflected on in these reflective inquiries threw you in to what people would call alpha or fluffy behaviours. Bear in mind that these behaviours can be beneficial in certain scenarios.

> ### *Reflective Inquiry: Uncovering your scripts*
>
> *Once you identify the disempowering situations that you want to shift, spend some time reflecting into the script you have written for each event:*
> - *What happened?*
> - *What meaning did you bring to the event?*
> - *How did it make you feel – and how does it make you feel when this script repeats in your life now?*
> - *What 'automatic' and unproductive behaviours do you display and what 'automatic' actions do you take when this script runs for you now?*
>
> *Reflect on the recent impacts of those actions.*

The value in this technique is that you can start to consciously decompose those scripts that do not empower you by enabling you to look at situations in which your behaviour is sub-optimal. There was a time when that script served you or protected you. There may be situations now where it no longer does – or it gets in the way.

Knowing what these scripts are, you will begin to appreciate that they are not true. They are just scripts you wrote at a certain time in your life based on a decision you made then - and then convinced yourself that the decision was the truth. You can now start to delete the old scripts and write new scripts that will lead to different, more productive behaviours and actions.

Inner Power Exercise: Writing new scripts

Pick the most disempowering situation that you identified in your reflective inquiries and start to consciously write a new script with new responses, new actions and behaviours to take when the source event happens that activates your script. You may like to use the following format:

The event/scenario that disempowers me is:

The new meaning I am bringing to this kind of event is:

The decision I will make in future as a result is:

This will make me feel:

demonstrate the following behaviours:

and take the following new actions:

In writing your new script, practice letting go of any disempowering feelings you had and make sure those are not in your new script.

Inner Power Exercise: Give yourself a KISS

For each situation you identified, look again at the strengths as well as the weaknesses of the behaviours you display and choose which behaviours and actions you are going to KEEP as they are, which you are going to IMPROVE, which you are going to STOP and which new ones you are going to START in specific situations.

Behaviours that I am going to:

Keep:

Improve:

Stop:

Start:

This is an on-going process and you want to start slowly and practice using this technique to start to break patterns that have had their time – freeing you up to new opportunities and to fully embrace the new future you have created for yourself. Start with the first script, and when you have caused a shift with this script, take on the next one.

Spend a month or two exploring your scripts before you embark on uncovering *Authentic You*.

Through all of this, remember that others usually have a much better opinion of you than you have of yourself. Know that in most instances, you are your harshest critic. My recommendation is that you find ways to give yourself a break and start to celebrate and appreciate all the amazing qualities that you as a woman bring to this planet of ours.

The environment in which to connect with *Authentic You*

There are so many distractions that to connect authentically with what really matters to you and the future you want for yourself based on what you care about requires that you *take yourself away from time to time*.

The perfect way to do this is to take yourself physically away – alone to somewhere you love – may be the mountains, a spa or a beautiful beach somewhere. You might prefer to do something you love – a real treat for you – perhaps a cookery course, golf, skiing, art or spiritual retreat. In this case, make sure whatever activity you choose gives you plenty of time for reflection and that it is in a climate, culture and environment that brings you to life and makes you shine. This is a time for you. A time for reflection and deep inquiry.

My recommendation is to take a week out like this at least once a year and ideally more, so that you can centre yourself and reflect on where you have been, where you are and where you are heading. You can then invest in yourself weekly – little but often to reflect on and reinforce your passion and purpose.

As I said, this would be the perfect way. I appreciate that life is not always perfect, so it may be that you actually need to create a retreat in your own home. A time and a space when you can arrange to be in a nurturing space within your own home when everything else is taken care of and you can just be with you. This reflective process will take some organising and may have to happen in shorter periods of say a couple of hours a week. It may take a bit longer than if you can get away for a week by yourself.

I'm here – now what?

So why would you choose to do this given all the hassle of having to organise everything and take time out?

It is because you as a woman need to ground yourself. Really connect with who you are and *what makes your heart sing*.

Reflective Inquiry: Your next trip down memory lane – a creative adventure

Once you are in this beautiful environment of time and space that is just for you, take some time to travel through your life again. This time appreciate who you are now and what you have accomplished. You may want to create a timeline starting from when you were born – looking at the high points (shine moments) and the low points (shrink moments) of your life. What did you learn in each of those instances? What qualities and values were either being fulfilled or missing that made it what it was for you?

Your timeline can be simply a line drawn on a piece of paper that represents time – along which you outline your journey so far, or a retrospective diary. Play with different forms. If you communicate best with words, your diary may take the traditional form; if you like pictures, you may want to build a photo album with a page for each year; or if you communicate best aurally, you may want to create and record poetry. You may be someone who loves technology and want to look through your personal video library to create a 30 seconds per year video montage of your life – the ecstatic moments of joy, the depths of sheer despair and everything in-between – sifted and sorted and captured as a foundation from which you can take stock, understand really who you have been and be ready to create a future.

This journey (if you invest yourself fully in it) will also be cathartic for you. Many people find memories that they want to address. They realise decisions they made as children or young adults that have either caused shrink or shine in their lives. It is useful to make a note of these. You may want to have conversations with people who were around when those decisions were made so that you can explore the situation with them and let go of anything that disempowers you.

The luxury of this self-inquiry is one of the best gifts you can give yourself. Make it a multi-sensory experience – use images, colours, textures, sounds and objects as you take your walk through memory lane.

Even if you have already done a lot of this kind of work, it is useful to take a fresh journey through your life at this point to celebrate who you have been and who you are now.

From here, you can start to take a really good look at you. Who are you as a woman… a professional… a daughter… a mother… a sister… a wife… a leader… a follower… a traveller… in each of the communities you engage with? What is really important for you? What is non-negotiable? What are showing up as your values? Who are you as Authentic You without the defence mechanisms, the internal dialogue, the alpha female or fluffy one? Start to appreciate the inner beauty of you and the authentic and valuable commitments you have in life.

2. A Clear Vision and Purpose for your Life

Now that you have this rich picture of who you are and what is important to you, you can start to look forward – what future would be consistent with what you are committed to in life?

> ***Reflective Inquiry: Your ideal future***
>
> *Next time you visit your personal retreat, take some time to look into the future: imagine yourself at 90, sitting in your favourite armchair, speaking with your favourite person in the world – sharing what you have accomplished in your life…what would you be most proud of? What would you be saying? What legacy will live on beyond you? Who have you made a lasting difference to? What are your greatest achievements?*

Really explore. Go wide. Speculate broadly. Remember to include your creation of life from now to 90. Use your beautiful nurturing space to sit in while you do this. Take your time. There is no rush. Let all the possible elements of your future surface. You may want to do this in one sitting, or let it emerge through regular immersions in your favourite space.

Your Core Values

The most critical gift you will give yourself through this deep reflection is an awareness of what is important to you. There are many tools available for you to work through a values evaluation. They generally start with a long list of what is important to you and narrow down to 3-5 words that represent the core of who you are – your non-negotiables in life. When you experience them in yourself and your life you feel the best you have ever been and when they are missing you feel really bad – rotten – and maybe even a failure. These values will move you forward when you let them be in your conscious life. When you are upset about something you can be sure that it is one of these values that has been violated. So make sure that you keep these close to you and create environments and opportunities that feed your core values.

Reflective Inquiry: Your values

Return to your 'Reflective Inquiry: Your next trip down memory lane – a creative adventure' and reflect again on your values. Create a long list of the values that have been at play during your life and see if you can bring this list down to 3-5 distinct words. This may take 2-3 iterations where the list gets iteratively shorter.

Next take some time now to reflect on which values and behaviours are driving you when people consider you an alpha female – when you are being results driven/scared of failing; and the values that are at play when they call you fluffy – when you are over-supportive or hiding away – when you are at your least assertive.

> *Keep these in your consciousness. Think about what your intentions are in those situations, give yourself another KISS (keep, Improve, stop start) and bring yourself to peace around those behaviours that you many not instantly love.*

My Core Values:

....
....
....
....
....
....
....
....
....
....
....

Behaviours I will:

Keep:

Improve:

Stop:

Start:

Once you can own your values and see the good in them, you will be able to shine – whether the behaviours are alpha, fluffy or somewhere in-between. Once you can accept them, your communication will be more authentic – you won't be trying to hide any behaviours – and people will be able to hear you with respect and trust.

Narrow in on what is important to you
It is now time to start tuning in to your passion and purpose in life. This is what drives you and what you believe you are here for. As you go through this exercise, know that the passion and purpose you are articulating is current – you are not stuck with it forever, and it may change as you progress. However, it will be your passion and purpose until it is fulfilled or no longer relevant at which time you can review and articulate a new passion and purpose.

The following Inner Power exercise is the first step in this process where I introduce the practice of listening from your head, heart and gut. When you do this, you are essentially giving your whole body and being a voice.

This is a practice that I will call on a few times in this book and a detailed guide to the practice is the first item in your Power Toolkit (Addendum 1)

> ### *Inner Power Exercise: Your priorities in life*
>
> *With your core values to hand, look back over your timeline to identify your shrink and shine moments: the shine moments when you felt invincible...like you were doing everything right and maybe had no idea how; the shrink moments...when you felt that you wanted the ground to open up and just swallow you – or when you just couldn't see how to get out of a situation you were stuck in.*
>
> *Make a list of all your shrink and shine moments, then go through them and add on who you were with, where you were, how old you were, what role you were playing (for example – were you a daughter, a student, a manager) and what was important to you at the time.*

My Shrink Moments:

Who	Where	Age	My Role	What Happened

My Shine Moments:

Who	Where	Age	My Role	What Happened

Reflective Inquiry: Your priorities

Look again at what is truly important to you – the people, the activities, the causes and the roles you play in life.

From this, identify your priorities right now and in the next 10 years or so.

Make sure you ask your head, heart and gut before you narrow in on the areas of life you want to focus on and which you want to let go of.

My Priorities in Life:

....

....

....

....

....

....

....

Bring it all together to form your Authentic Purpose and your Third Chapter

> ### *Reflective Inquiry: Your Purpose in life*
>
> *On a completely different occasion – and perhaps in a completely different nurturing space, answer this question for yourself: "What Ding am I going to leave on the planet when I am no longer here?" These are the words of the genius Steve Jobs. Are you wanting to leave a ding on that scale? That would be great. However, your ding may be focused on your contribution to your family, community, company – or maybe the people you mentor and develop throughout your career.*

Your authentic purpose can't be too small AND it can't be too big. You will know when you have hit it when you can feel it in your gut, the ends of your finger-tips tingle and you are excited beyond words about it. You may be afraid to speak about it to anyone else. That's ok. When you find it, share it anyway. The more people you share it with, the more your environment will support you in making it happen.

You will find that there is something unexpected and unimaginable that happens when you get your purpose clear. Somehow opportunities relating to your purpose start to show up. It is as if you create a magnetic field that attracts support for your fulfilling on your purpose. You just need the courage and the presence of mind to spot those opportunities and then act on them.

> ### *Inner Power Exercise: Your Third Chapter*
>
> *Once you have your authentic purpose it in your head, heart and gut, sleep on it. Make sure you keep a beautiful, high quality piece of paper (at least A4 and ideally A3), together with your favourite pen right by your bedside before you go to sleep. You will need it in the morning.*
>
> *First thing when you wake up the next day is take your pen and paper and write your stream of consciousness about your life in 10 years time. Put yourself at a point 10 years from now. Visualise it briefly and then let your pen flow. This will become the third chapter of your life.*
>
> *Once you have written your third chapter, read it through and choose it powerfully – with no guilt. Know that you will be going forward with this future – overcoming fear and moving away from procrastination.*

In the past, my last statement would have been considered to be 'woo-woo' thinking. However, there is now a body of evidence coming from the very logical brain science research community that indicates that our energetics (such as 'positive thinking', for example) impact our experience, the experience of people around us and even physical events in our world. You will find some references to scientific research in this area in the Power Toolkit.

So my recommendation is that you embrace the opportunity of creating your purpose to cause and own your future rather putting it down to luck or waiting for luck to find you.

My Third Chapter

3. Bring your Purpose to Life

The best place to start bringing your purpose to life is where you already shine. The next reflective inquiry explores the environmental elements and people that support you and your third chapter as well as those that are more challenging for you. We then look at structures through which you can start to realise your purpose and make sure it happens.

> ***Reflective Inquiry:***
> *Start by taking a look at your current environment. What elements of your current life support you in fulfilling your third chapter – and which have had their time?*
>
> *Give yourself another KISS – this time in the context of your environment. Which elements are you going to keep, improve or stop? Which alpha and fluffy behaviours will support you? What will you start doing to make it work for the future?*

In my environment, going forward I will

Keep:

Improve:

Stop:

Start:

Behaviours I will:

      Keep:

      Improve:

      Stop:

      Start:

What currently works? What needs to change? Take a look at your team members – what are their passions, values and purpose. What are their strengths and weaknesses? What opportunities are they going for? How is all that congruent with where you are heading – and where is it a threat? How can you empower them to develop and succeed? How can they do the same for you?

Similarly look at your management chain – what are their aspirations? Do you fit in with that? How can you support their success? Do their values align with yours?

Who are the other stakeholders you have to account for at work? Create a list of all your stakeholders and make sure you keep that refreshed. You will be referring to it as you work through this book.

When it comes to work, start with you and your role.

What works Already?	What I am going to Change	Actions I will Take
	STAFF	
	MANAGEMENT CHAIN	
	OTHER STAKEHOLDERS	

Is the organisation you are working in consistent with the future you are committed to for yourself? Do their values – their positioning politically, economically, socially and technologically fit with the future you are creating for yourself? What opportunities do you see for yourself and how do they fit in with your new purpose?

Opportunities that match my Purpose:

....

....

....

....

....

....

....

....

Having reviewed all of this, identify for yourself where you stand out as contributing value to your team, your management chain and your organisation.

Make sure to do a non-work check-in. It is important to take an integrated view of your whole life. The old concept of work/life balance is somewhat out-dated in today's environment. For example, many of us listen to podcasts while we are doing household chores; we have a great opportunity to practice empathy and listening when we are with our children. So take some time to look at your life from a 'whole life' perspective. How does your new future fit in with your home, your life stage, your children and parents, your community commitments and the dynamics in play with your relationships? What will you have to manage? How can you influence and be supported through the changes you are about to make?

Make a list of what differentiates you at work – whether that is in your current environment – or a new environment that you are choosing to move to.

Ultimately, what you are looking to accomplish through this inquiry is whether and how your current environment enables your purpose and future to be fulfilled in a way that has integrity for you and in a way that differentiates you.

Where I already stand out:

Have Goals and a Plan to track your progress

You are now ready to set goals for yourself through which you can use to measure the level to which you are living by your passion and purpose and fulfilling on your third chapter. In today's fast moving environment, you can hold your 10-year future in your mind and visualise it, but the biggest value will come from having goals for each forthcoming year of your life that you set for yourself at the end of the preceding year. This will take you in a manageable way towards your 10 year vision.

A practice that I take on for my life is to take time over the Christmas break to reflect on the year that has just gone by and start to think about the year that lies ahead. Again, there are many methods for this part of the journey. My favourite is the 'Best Year Yet' process originally developed by Jinny Ditzler. Ditzler's process takes me through a holistic review of my life. I then give myself a KISS by looking at what practices, behaviours and actions I am going to Keep, Improve, Stop and Start. Finally, I set myself 3-5 breakthrough goals for the year and create a 'plan on a page' for steering me throughout the year. I use the term 'breakthrough' advisedly and what I mean by that is explained in your Power Toolkit.

If left there, this exercise is at risk of being no more than a nice idea – or dying like any other New Year's resolution. The secret to making these goals sustainable is to break them down into quarterly milestones, daily targets and weekly actions. The Power Toolkit has a useful section that talks you through the process of creating inspiring 'Breakthrough Goals' and a visual 'Plan on a Page that will support you in following through.

You also need to be very effective in managing when it does not go quite as planned. This is when your 'self-talk' takes over and can sabotage you. Know that if you have set truly breakthrough goals, you may not achieve all your actions, targets, milestone or goals. This is not another reason for you to feel guilty or afraid. If at the end of the period you have not achieved your goal, look at what you did or didn't do / have or didn't have to make it happen and build this into the next cycle of achieving your goal.

Even with great breakthrough goals and a solid plan on a page, there are many people you will need to get on board. As with many negotiations, you may not get everything you want. But at least you will know what you are aiming for - from which you can choose where you want to compromise. It is critical that you ensure you are choosing the compromises you make and not be driven by guilt or creating new resentments. Again, this may require significant effort and soul-searching from you.

As you may be experiencing by now, taking time to plan your future is not an overnight affair. It takes a lot of soul searching; creativity, dedication and effort to create and fulfil on your third chapter.

This whole process takes a lot of courage, so I urge you not to start it if you do not see how this is worth doing. You may want to find a 'birth partner' to support you in giving birth to *Authentic You*. Your birth partner must be someone who is outside your immediate environment and can give you unbiased feedback. It could be someone you have met through networking or a mentor or a coach. Make sure it is someone you would trust your life with – because this is your life that you are putting at stake. You are putting your life at stake for a future that really matters to you – so that the rest of your life is a real expression of who you are in the world and what you want to contribute.

As you start to draw your third chapter, be aware that things can change. You can always adapt your goals and plan, but the main thing is to choose powerfully, free of guilt and give yourself sufficient time to test it out before giving up on it.

Recruit a Virtual Board to Steer and Support You

Many women I meet worry about having to network – believing that men are better at it than women. They feel they are disadvantaged and missing out because of this.

The trick to networking is not going to lots of meetings, but identifying the key network of allies who have your back. These are trusted advisors who understand your contribution to the world of work. Some of them will be people of influence that you can consult, share concerns with and whom you can depend on to be your champions. They can put you in touch with the right people and put you forward when they hear about the right opportunities. You also want your virtual board to have a network of experts and a network of introducers.

You will come to realise that you don't have to be alone and you don't have to do it all yourself as many women in our surveys seemed to believe to be true. Through your virtual board, you will find the resources, encouragement and support to move beyond these constraints to "I am ready now" and go for what really matters to you. Never forget how much people love contributing to each other.

The people on your Virtual Board are people who understand you and what you have to offer. They support you in understanding the 'invisible rules' you will find at work. You will learn to appreciate that invisible rules are not intentional – they have just been in your blind spot until now. This will enable you to own learning the rules from them rather than being at the impact of not knowing what they are.

Strategy Gem:

Take out and refresh your stakeholder list. Add anyone who you will need to have as a stakeholder in order to fulfil on your purpose. From this list, look at who could be your guardian angel at work? Who will look out for opportunities for you to progress? Who will teach you the invisible rules at work and support you in managing the 'old boys club'. When it looks like there is no one on earth you can turn to, who will understand you? These will generally be people who have an interest in supporting you. Your value exchange with them is more about being appreciated for their contribution and seeing you achieve your full potential at work and in life.

Scream Partner:

Who can you go to when you just want to SCREAM? Find yourself a scream champion. A few things to be aware of in creating the relationship with your 'scream' champion. It is critical to set it up well. Let them know that you are approaching them for this role because you trust them and feel free to be your authentic self – warts and all with them. Share the work you have done so far – particularly your alpha and fluffy sides so that they can be aware of how you might behave in tough situations. This will prepare them for what they might have to deal with. Give them full permission to 'handle' you in those situations. See if you can create it as a two-way street so that you are available to them for the same purpose.

Find out from them how they would like you to contact them when you need to access them as a member of your scream team. For example, it may not be practical for many people during work hours, so how will you manage that? Do you have people who are not currently working who will understand you and your situation enough to add value in these conversations? These are the most sensitive board roles you will be setting up, so make sure you set them up well and with the right people. Agree boundaries for confidentiality, compassion and forgiveness with them and keep those boundaries in the conscious realm for both of you as much as possible.

Knowledge and Skills:
Look at the skills and knowledge required to fulfil on your future. Where are the gaps in your knowledge? At this point you can adopt one of two strategies. You can either try to learn everything you need to know and be a perfectionist – a trait that has held many women back – or you can identify who you know who has the skills and knowledge you will need to draw upon in the future. Add these people to your virtual board. Knowing you have access to these experts will give you the confidence to take opportunities you might otherwise pass by – or wait until you know exactly how to do it and that you are ready. In setting up the relationships, look at what you have to offer them that would be of value. Is there an area of knowledge that is important to them with which you can reciprocate? Will they want to be paid for sharing their knowledge? This is a sensitive area. The success in setting up these relationships will be the depth to which you clarify reciprocity and value exchange in the relationship.

> ***Influencers and Champions:***
> *Don't forget to think about the people who can make relevant introductions on your behalf. Who do you need to develop professional relationships with in order to fulfil on the purpose you have created? If you do not know them directly, who do you know who would love to make the connections for you? Many people get a sense of contribution and satisfaction from being able to support people they value, so give them the opportunity to do that. These people often show up where you put yourself out there to give back to causes you care about… perhaps through mentoring in the community or your company's CSR initiative. These are people who could evolve into sponsors and become your career guardians.*
>
> *Your virtual board exists to fill the sponsorship, network and skills gaps that you need to fill in order to fulfil on your purpose. Once you have a long list of people for your virtual board, review and choose no more than 3 for each category (scream, skills and knowledge, influence and champions). Look both at your current contacts as well as people you may need to find. Remember that this is not about including everyone who likes you.*

You can now start to have conversations with your potential Virtual Board members. Share with them what you are creating – your purpose and who else is on your virtual board. Have conversations with them to clarify why you are inviting them to join – what their commitment will be, why you chose them and what they believe they can contribute and gain from being on your Board.

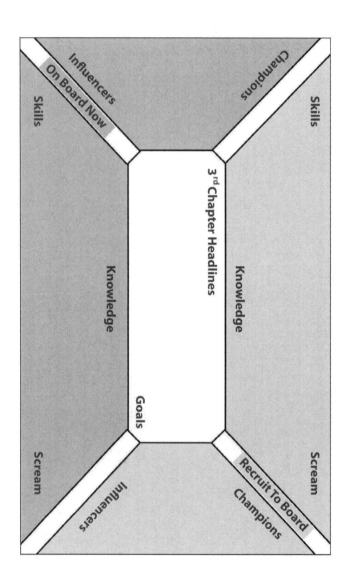

One thing to understand is that the Virtual Board does not meet as a traditional Board would. The members on your Virtual Board team are essentially your super-network. They are people you may meet with individually or in small groups once a quarter to check in. You may select and agree with a couple of them to have more regular conversations, but you want to make sure that the commitment on them is light and mainly advisory from time to time, in a mentoring capacity. Create a regular contact plan with each board member and aim to stick to it. However, accept that these are usually busy people and may have to cancel/rearrange at short notice. Avoid the pitfall of thinking they cancelled and therefore don't care/don't have time for you or anything else your internal dialogue may tell you. If appointments get missed, make sure that you gracefully rearrange and acknowledge the value they continue to provide.

There have been times in my career where members of my virtual board kept me straight and created opportunities for me. In my very first position at BT, there were times when I found the 'civil service' mindset of the recently privatised organisation stifling and lacking imagination. Shortly after I joined, Phil joined our Division. He had a spark in his eyes that told me he was up for having an impact. I quickly identified him as someone I wanted to work with. He was my manager's manager and while I would not bypass my manager, I found that I had more of a rapport with Phil. He guided me through many of my early successes in my standards, consultancy, training and quality roles. He was sponsored by BT to study for a business studies degree and shared a lot of what he learned with me. Over time, as I proved myself he put me forward to be sponsored for my MBA. I know that without him, I would not have progressed at the pace I did in my early career. Phil, if you are reading this – my eternal thanks to you.

Then there is Rik, an incredible, energetic, thoughtful and compassionate leader who always saw the best in me and coached me to transform the worst in me. With him, I got to really be myself and share what was in the way of my performance. Through these conversations, I learned more about myself as well as the world of business. He would put me forward for opportunities at work and also let me know when I was sailing close to the edge or not fulfilling on my brief.

Such internal advocates are critical for our sanity and our antennae should always be looking out for the Riks and Phils at work.

To find virtual board members outside the workplace you might want to consider your broader network. One of my clients is very involved with her religious group and has only recently started sharing with them about her work. As a result, she has found people who want to contribute to her because of their experience of her at the church gatherings and her credibility and integrity in those situations. Another started to look at her family and community members – realising that this is a source of valuable knowledge and connections.

You may also consider volunteering your time as a mentor or virtual board member to others. This gives you an opportunity to contribute back and widen the network of people you have access to. Thoughtfully select a mentoring opportunity that is close to your heart and consistent with your purpose.

In my case, I have mentored with the Princes Trust and students at London Business School because I believe it is important to give back. This fulfils me and connects me with entrepreneurs and future business leaders who will in turn value my contribution to them. I also mentor with Mosaic – an organisation set up by HRH Prince Charles to open up opportunities for school age children in deprived, inner city areas by widening their horizons and learning business skills. As well as filling my heart with joy to be with these children as their eyes light up when they see new opportunities, I have met other inspiring mentors who enrich my life.

Find a cause you are moved by that you want to impact when you choose your mentoring roles. For me, it is the empowerment of women in business. As such, I take on projects such as designing the FastForward15 mentoring scheme and coaching business leaders who are providing their time free of charge to mentor up-and-coming women in the hospitality, conference and events sectors. Although 78% of the working population in this sector are women, less than 10% of senior leaders are female. My motivation is purely to cause a shift for women in this sector by contributing my time, however, the relationships I am building are fulfilling and some of the business leaders have engaged me to support development of people in their businesses. The key is to go into it with a pure intention. If good things come out of it – which they will if your intentions are good – that is a brilliant bonus.

4. Make it Work – Techniques for overcoming blocks to keep it alive

As you head towards fulfilling on your purpose and letting *Authentic You* show up, many situations, people and events will appear to sabotage you. It is critical to keep yourself on track and deal with your 'self-talk' powerfully.

Here are some techniques that will enable you to keep your plan alive.

Top Tip 1: Choose your Battles

Use Strategies to Cause Change Where it is Important to YOU and Let the Other Complaints Go. Don't Let Them Hinder You

Accept that some things may never change and don't let that disempower you.

This does not mean that you should give up on your standards and values or stop doing what you are doing to cause the change. It just means that you will not be distracted by the complaint.

What it will enable you to do is pick your battles and not be disempowered by what is going on around you.

Use some of the strategies here to support you in causing that change for yourself and those you care about (at work and outside).

However, don't let negative 'self-talk' fill your head and stop you from focusing on what is really important to you.

Top Tip 2: Develop a constructive approach to conflict

Most organisations are designed to thrive on competition. This can lead to situations of conflict. What I find with many of my female clients as opposed to my male clients is that they avoid conflict wherever possible. They see conflict as a bad thing and this suppresses their self-expression and freedom to operate. They then stew on the conflict situation in which they did not allow themselves to speak up and some form of less than useful behaviour shows up out of context in a totally different situation and reflects badly on them.

Most men on the other hand have a positive attitude to conflict. It is seen as a way of driving for the best solution. They will say what they have to and then move on – they don't hold on to the conflict and let it fester into resentment. This keeps their mind free to focus on what there is to deal with in the present rather than bring emotions that do not support their objectives.

It may be useful for you to look at how you respond in conflict situations. Are you someone who generally avoids, accommodates, compromises, competes or collaborates? There is no right way to respond, but it is useful for you to develop an ability to respond with each of these different ways at choice rather than be thrown to one of them. For example, when the conflict situation is not that important to you, it would be fine to avoid the conflict. In a promotion situation, it would be useful to compete. In many cases – especially where time is not critical, you might choose to collaborate, whereas when you are time bound with what looks like an impasse, you might compromise. In a situation where you can achieve your outcome whilst providing what the other wants at no cost to you, you might accommodate.

Developing the dimensions in which you manage conflict will assist you in showing up as your authentic self and standing for your purpose, promise and proposition in the face of no-agreement.

Top Tip 3: Manage your *Inner Diva* – accept the Authentic You

Very often, people tell me that there are actual circumstances that are stopping them from progressing… the economy… a lack of time… a lack of money… the recession… their staff… but as I dig deeper, I find that it is usually the range of conversations they are having inside their head about their ability to build their operation, lead their teams and belief in their own capability. The same goes for situations in which they complain to me about the impact of other peoples' behaviour and attitudes towards them that they say prevents them from realising their full potential.

We have often heard that it is important to be authentic at work if one is to be a high performing leader. Being authentic requires a deep under-standing of yourself and who you are.

This authenticity will help ensure that you show up as a credible leader. Not as someone who stands in the wings or gets nudged off by someone else. Nor as the ambitious, results focused driver who pays scant attention to peoples' needs or feeling.

However, being true to yourself is sometimes hard to achieve and in stressful situations, the flip sides of our personalities often come to the fore, exposing what might metaphorically be called your *'Inner Diva'*. The *'Inner Diva'* is a metaphor for the 'character' that lives inside all of us. In work situations, she comes out in moments of absolute brilliance as well as moments of absolute darkness. You may not like this metaphor, but it does its job.

There is no hiding from the *Inner Diva*. She appears during your 'shine' moments: those times when you do something outstanding or brilliant. She also emerges during your 'shrink' moments: when you display behaviours you would rather keep to yourself - times when you are angry or say the wrong thing and offend people – either verbally and with force using your alpha characteristics, or revert to passive aggression and your fluffy features.

It may be that you often try to suppress your *Inner Diva*, thinking that it will reflect negatively on you if you let her out. This is a bit like fast cooking in a pressure cooker. Once the stopper is released you get a head of steam that was not expected from looking at the still outside of the pan. Like the jet of steam from a pressure cooker, your suppressed *Inner Diva* will surely erupt at some point - usually in a moment of stress. Either your alpha will have a tantrum or your fluffy will become petulant, shutdown or disappear.

Knowing and accepting the *Inner Diva* is the first step to being ok with her. Allowing every part of your character to be as it is rather than trying to suppress aspects that you think others may not like or approve of is the beginning of being totally authentic in the workplace. Interestingly, when you truly accept who you are, you find that those shrink causing characteristics do not show up in quite such an inappropriate way.

> ### *Inner Power Exercise: Get to know your Inner Diva*
>
> *A simple way to identify your Inner Diva is to again look back through the story of your life and think about people you have been compared with in the past. What are their characteristics when they are operating in shrink and shine modes?*
>
> *A more light-hearted way for you to understand your Inner Diva is to play a game with friends and colleagues to identify each other's Inner Divas. In this moment of playfulness, a lot of truth comes out. This good-humoured research will help you clarify more about your characteristics and how others perceive you.*
>
> *You might also like to draw insights by identifying famous people. Which famous personality are you most like when you are at your best and when you are at the other extreme?*
>
> *Ask yourself: 'what characteristics do people admire about this person and speak highly of?' 'What negative press do they get?' How do all these opinions about her apply to me? 'How does she handle her good and bad press?' 'What can I learn from her?'*
>
> *Having matched yourself to a famous Diva, think about a Diva who really inspires you and repeat the reflection.*

These inner power exercises enable you to know your positive behaviours that lead to outstanding results. You can then begin to own your greatness rather than attribute good results to chance. You also understand more about the behaviours that make you shrink so that you can manage them more effectively.

> ### *Reflective Inquiry:*
>
> *A powerful way to manage shrink moments is to visualise what happens just before the actual shrink moment. What thoughts were you having? What was said that triggered the shrink? How did you feel just before and just after? Where did you feel it? What behaviours and actions could you now start developing that you can apply just before shrink moments arise in future? By consciously identifying and practicing these behaviours and actions, you can act on the impending shrink moment before it happens.*

With a raised level of self-awareness and insight you can increase your personal impact and influence, begin to understand what you have accomplished in moments of exceptional performance and also effectively manage when things are about to go south.

Knowing and understating your *Inner Diva* will help you shine from within. Make sure to use its energy to shine in a way that communicates your contribution at work.

Once you have mastered the *Inner Diva* for yourself, you can use this metaphor with people at work and gently support them in identifying their *Inner Divas* as well as their shrink and shine moments. You will then have a powerful tool for building more effective teams that make a valuable contribution to the performance of your organisation.

Top Tip 4: Manage your 'Self-Talk'

We have explored in some depth how self-talk can spiral into disempowerment and become a major barrier to your progress. A number of techniques have been developed to support people in dealing with negative self-talk.

My favourite technique for causing a state change in my 'Self-Talk' is to use the script method we discussed earlier in this Chapter. It will enable you to deeply explore old scripts and write new scripts that move you forward.

Other useful techniques include: Reframing, Mindfulness, NLP methods such as anchoring and meditative techniques such as Ho-o-pono-pono. Brief guidance on how you can use these techniques can be found in your Power Toolkit.
You can use these techniques, as well as widely available breathing techniques to restore yourself to a peaceful space, and address some of the challenges you face (such as those identified in Chapter 2).

When you come up against something that hits a raw nerve or something that makes you feel uncomfortable. That is the perfect time to practice these techniques. The trick is to catch that situation and know that you can't perform at your best when you are in that space, and then apply some of the techniques discussed here.

Top Tip 5: Invest in Developing the New Skills you need as a leader at work

As you progress through your career, the things that make you successful change – from knowledge based and technical skills to leadership and management skills. Make sure you stay relevant and develop new skills such as: strategic visioning, managing performance, articulate communication, collaboration, effective delegation, empowering and leading your team, shaping rather than doing, being flexible and able to reprioritise for the benefit of the business.

Whilst many skills can be 'insourced' through your networks, these core leadership skills are essential to today's leaders and will support you in achieving your third chapter.

Chapter 7 – Manage Your Profile: Your Promise and Proposition

What makes you stand out?
When I was 9 years old, my grandmother used a really great metaphor that pushed me to take action. I invite you to try this on. She used to tell me: "Ishreen, there is no point in having a pretty frock that costs a lot of money if you just keep it in the cupboard…you have to wear it and go out so that people can see it." Her wisdom still brings tears to my eyes. I bet you already know that you are good at your job and good at learning what you need to when you need to. So, I invite you to go for it and get yourself known by those that matter to your success. Don't hold back. Combine this with those great emotional intelligence skills that you already apply to doing great work and apply both to support you in fulfilling on your aspirations.

Regardless of age, regardless of position, regardless of the business we happen to be in, all of us need to understand the importance of branding. We are CEOs of our own companies: Me Inc. To be in business today, our most important job is to be head marketer for the brand called You." – Tom Peters, Aug/Sep 1997, The Fast Company Magazine.

This famous quote from business guru Tom Peters illustrates that it is essential for you to understand and communicate the value you add to key stakeholders – even if you may not be someone who likes to talk about yourself.

As you will have read in the recap of our research findings, many women believe that doing a good job and delivering excellent results with a team that has a high degree of respect and support for you should be enough for your manager to spot your talent and put you forward for promotion.

Some women have hit the jackpot and are fortunate enough to be sponsored in this way. Unfortunately, though the vast majority of up-lines are either more focused on advancing their own careers or snowed under delivering on their account-abilities, so it is unrealistic to depend on them to sponsor you. It is now time for you to OWN IT and cause that sponsorship for yourself.

For this to happen, you will need a clear message that communicates your promise and proposition, be able to demonstrate your credibility and create an emotional connection that motivates others to listen to how you can benefit them, their team and the organisation.

With this message you will be able to create the impact you want rather than live by the opinions of others.

Often people don't proactively manage the perceptions others have of them. They carry on day to day – doing a great job, but not paying attention to the impressions they leave with others.

Once you have a clear purpose and plan you can start to create the messages that let you influence what others say about you and create opportunities for yourself that move you in the direction of your breakthrough goals.

In effect, you need to define *Authentic You* – your Professional Brand.

Your Professional Brand is a function of who you are, what you want to be known for and who people perceive you to be. It is a conscious and proactive manifestation of the identity you project as opposed to the passive image that people mostly end up with. More importantly, it is your promise to your stake-holders - what they can expect from you and how you differentiate yourself from your 'competition.'

For many of you, this may conjure up thoughts of distasteful marketing and exaggerated self-promotion. If this is the case, I suggest you look seriously at what I am recommending here. I am not saying that you should create a piece of fiction for others to hear and be convinced by. What I am saying is that in the interests of owning the fulfilment of your aspirations. You need to present yourself to others as the "best you" so that they have the best chance of knowing, supporting and choosing you.

So why would you take time to do this?

Firstly, if you don't cultivate in others a knowledge of who you really are, they will. Their version of who you are will create a perception about you that will become a reality in the minds of those you need to influence. In some cases, that may not work in your favour.

You have certain skills and capabilities to contribute. It is your job to assist others to know and care about what those are, what value you are adding and what you have to offer.

The first impression people have of you is usually visual.

You may think that starting here is 'dumbing down' the conversation about your brand. It is an unfortunate fact that your physical appearance – dress and body language represents the vast majority of what communicates about you.

For example, one thing that stands out about me is that I cover my hair. This is a choice I made some time ago, but was not sure how it would work in a professional environment. I tried out some traditional styles, but it did not fit with my personality – even before I thought about a professional setting. I played with a few different options and finally settled on using batik squares. These held a strong cultural connection with me as well given that they were made in Sri Lanka. This seemed to work well for me and I have a good collection of elegant batik scarves in different colours. One day, someone whose opinion I value said to me "Ishreen, you know your scarf is not consistent with the rest of your clothes… you look so professional in everything else you wear - and then your scarf looks like you are on holiday." This set me back a little because I was very proud of my scarves. However, I let in what she said and had a few plain scarves made for my more 'serious' activities. I still wear my batik scarves a lot, but what I do is think about when a plain scarf would be more appropriate. Of course, lucky me to have people who will give me this kind of advice, but the main thing is that I let her comment in, considered it and did not follow it blindly – I included it in my branding conversation with myself.

So what first impression does your physical appearance create?

Reflective Inquiry: Your Physical Brand

As a quick audit, one morning just before you leave for work, stand in front of a full length mirror and ask yourself what impression the person looking back at you creates.

She may appear powerful, confident and professionally dressed.

Is she a little scary?

She may look as if she dressed in a real hurry and her shoes are not that well polished...her clothes don't exactly match well and she is a bit unkempt...

She may look very glamorous – dressed in designer clothes and high heels..

...what is your reflection saying to you about you?

Take a note for yourself of the first impression your visual appearance has on you. Each one of the above statements may be valid depending on your role. The question to reflect on is whether your look is consistent with your purpose, promise and proposition. If not, you may want to speak with a professional style consultant to make sure how you look fits with what you are looking to accomplish.

What my reflection says about me:

....

....

....

Make sure you put aside some time to reflect on your gestures, body language, your tone of voice and the language you use to communicate. Look at where all of this fits with your purpose promise and proposition. Is there anything to develop yourself in or work on here?

Inner Power Exercise: How you make others feel

How do you make people feel when they are around you? Do they mostly shrink or shine around you? Who are the people you cause to shine? Look at where they fit in with your purpose, promise and proposition. How about the ones who tend to shrink around you? How can you change your behaviours to enable them to shine?

Look at how people benefit from working with you.

Reflecting on these aspects of who you are will provide a rich context for developing your Professional Brand.

Defining Authentic You

Having spent some time self-reflecting on the brand you currently project, you can start to define *Authentic You*. Include everything that is consistent with your purpose, promise and proposition. Ask others what they value about you. You could do this through informal interviews or through a more formal structure such as a 360 evaluation where 5-7 people who report to you and those you report to complete an online leadership survey about what they think you are good at and what you could improve on.

All this will inform your SWOT analysis (strengths that create a competitive advantage and weakness that need to be managed with respect delivering on your promise and proposition as well as the opportunities you can benefit from and threats you face). This is a simple exercise that has been used in business and branding for many years. It will bring clarity to *Authentic You*. Make sure your SWOT is framed in the context of your purpose, promise and proposition.

In defining *Authentic You* and how you communicate who you are, it is critical to account for the fact that people are busy and don't always have time to listen to the detail. This is where your 'brand essence' comes in. The brand essence communicates the essence of who you are. It is a quick and memorable statement that describes who you are, what you have to offer and what makes you unique.

Refer back to your reflections on what is clearly identifiable about you that makes you stand out – physical, verbal, non-verbal, voice, skills, personality and behaviours. Identify which of these are most relevant to your purpose, promise and proposition. How will they help people relate positively to you and what you can provide?

Look back at your list of key stakeholders who will contribute to and benefit from your purpose, promise and proposition. Identify what it will provide for them.

Think about what is important to them and how you would communicate your purpose, promise and proposition to them – what words you would use and what tone of voice.

Think about how your personality affects the experience people have with you – how you make people feel, how they benefit from working with you and what words they use to describe you.

Once you have defined *Authentic You*, it is critical that you find different ways to take it out into your stakeholder community and that you own that brand in how you do that.

A good next step is to share *Authentic You* with your virtual board, get their feedback – and just as I did with the person who generously advised me about my scarf choice, make sure you listen to their contribution, reflect deeply and decide if and how you will incorporate their feedback into *Authentic You*.

What is critical through all of this is to 'manage the diva within'. One thing you can be sure of is that the negative side of your Diva will start speaking very loudly as you articulate and start sharing *Authentic You*. So make sure you find ways to stay connected to your strengths so that you minimise time spent on unproductive conversations about what you still need to improve. Keep letting the Diva know that you have this handled and it will all work out well.

Strategy Gem: Articulating your Professional Brand

It is often useful to collate this into three statements:

Brand Essence: A short statement of about 5 words that clearly communicates who you are and that inspires you about who you are. This should be simple and memorable. It should be authentic and not 'spin'; however, it needs to communicate the essence of who you are.

Elevator Pitch: A 30 second communication that elaborates on the Brand Essence and acts as a teaser – providing enough information and piquing your listeners interest sufficiently to invite you to a longer meeting.

Positioning Statement: A more detailed (5-10 minute) communication that contains the key elements of Authentic You and acts as the source of all other communications you create to let people know who you are and what value you add.

These statements must connect at all levels with your target audience – head, heart and gut. Review your communications to make sure that it appeals to the emotions as well as intellect and is designed to cause a next action.

What do you stand for?
You will already have reflected on what is important to you when you developed your purpose, promise and proposition.

Before you look at how you will communicate your promise and proposition to others, it is useful to pause and become clear again about what you stand for. This will enable you to maintain your integrity and authenticity in communication.

Make sure you know what is important to you in terms of your values, commitments, purpose and goals.

Some up-lines and teams may not operate in a way that is consistent with your values. Think seriously about whether you are willing to align with their values before you take a position with them because chances are you will not be able to bring them round to operating by your values. Alternatively, you could negotiate with them to give you an exception from certain norms – but be aware that this will exclude you from some aspects of the team. You will then have to manage your inner diva and let her know that this was a choice you made so no permission to get resentful.

If you value work life balance for example, and have a commitment to being at all your child's sports events, be clear with yourself about that. Don't pretend that is not the case in looking for your next opportunity – and don't take a position that assumes you will put work first at every turn without negotiating what is important to you.

Likewise, if travel and adventure at work is important to you, don't sell out and take a mainly desk based job.

It is also important for you to know your boundaries about how much you are willing to share with others and how much access you are willing to provide for others. Take some time to reflect on what are reasonable, safe and permissible ways for people to access you and what you will do and say if they step outside those boundaries.

Examples of boundaries you might want to consider include: how much of your home life you think is appropriate to share with your work colleagues and what impact that will have on your Professional Brand; or how much work you are willing to take home; what times you are going to work if required in the evenings for global calls. As a part of creating your strategy for managing situations where your boundaries are violated by others, reflect back on how your inner diva responds and what you need to manage about her.

I have discussed at length the importance of being true to yourself and communicating authentically. In order to do this, you need to be honest about your values and ideas. There is of course a health warning here. You are managing your brand, so it would not work to put your mind on loudspeaker, but rather communicate in a way that is responsible, sensitive and for mutual benefit.

As you develop your ability to communicate authentically you will demonstrate a level of consistency where your words and actions align with your core message. This is one of the 3Cs of Professional Branding. The others are clarity (communicating a clear promise, proposition, personality and story) and constancy (showing that *Authentic You* is dependable and demonstrable over time). A key access for achieving this is to know what you stand for and value in yourself and others.

Time for you to Shine
Having thought through and clarified *Authentic You* it is time to get you ready to communicate your promise and proposition to your stakeholders.

Imagine for a minute that you are creating a film of your life. Look back on the third chapter that you wrote as a part of developing your promise.

Who would you choose to play your leading lady? Think of a famous actress who you think would play that role most accurately. Look at what qualities she has that makes her a good fit?

Look again at your appearance. Is it a match for your value proposition? Review your level of confidence, check in with your body language. Make sure that your accoutrements are a match for you as your leading lady – your phone, your car, the way you dress. These are all things that will form an impression in the mind of your audience, so it is critical that they match your promise and proposition – otherwise people will not trust it or you.

My favourite example of this is one of my clients who works in child protection. She was always well turned out and professional looking. Her suits were well cut and tailored to her shape by an excellent tailor. She was someone who prided herself on her compassion and being able to connect with people. However, she did not understand why in a certain situation people did not engage fully with her. Working with a style consultant, she identified that her jackets made her appear different from this particular audience – less approachable. She took the style consultant's advice to wear cardigans instead of jackets in that environment and found that almost immediately this particular audience let her in more willingly and she could communicate in her usual, connected way with them.

Pay attention to your voice. Does it support your value proposition? Does it speak at a 10 out of 10? Look at what it is about your voice that is consistent with your promise and purpose and how you can let those aspects shine. Also look at what is missing. Is it the volume or steadiness? Is it the pitch? You may want to engage a voice coach to support you in projecting your voice if it is not on point for your leading lady. A voice coach will enable you to let go of the disempowering conversations that are in the way for you to communicate your authentic self fully.

Finally, think about your online persona. Make sure that your LinkedIn profile communicates your promise, proposition and personality. Make sure your Facebook and other non-professional social media have appropriate communications – or if you want freedom to communicate on Facebook limit your Facebook friends to your social circles. It is important that your social media is updated regularly to keep people engaged with your proposition.

Your job here is to develop and present a persona that reflects the true you in your best light.

Chapter 8 – Manage Your Profile: Get your Message Out There

Identify your audience
Once you have your proposition drafted – it is time to share it with your advocates.

However, before you start to share your new vision, purpose, promise and proposition it is essential for you to understand who your key stakeholders are and map them based on importance and accessibility.

It is useful to approach your target audience from a broad perspective and narrow down to key stakeholders. The following approach will guide you in identifying your target audience at different levels. You can refer back to any previous stakeholder maps and lists you have in parallel.

Strategy Gem: Your stakeholders

1. Start by brainstorming all the people and organisations you know that could benefit from or contribute to the success of your purpose in life and your proposition. Look through your own personal supply chain to identify who supplies you with what you need to deliver on your proposition and who are the potential consumers of what you have to offer? Also look at who is funding your proposition – who brings wealth into your life. This includes not only the organisation that pays your wages, but also your team and up-line; your professional and personal networks, your family and friends; where you go for your spiritual regeneration, your health and fitness, your neighbourhood, your children's schools.

Take time to create a picture – a visual representation (words, drawings or photos) of all the people in your life who contribute to your success – either directly or indirectly. These are the stakeholders in your life.

2. Who is your audience? Who needs to hear your purpose, promise and proposition? In some cases, these will be people you can name, in others it will be a function or a position you need to have access to.

As you look over the picture you have created, reflect on each person – how could they contribute to your purpose and proposition? How could they benefit from it? Find a way to make these people easily identifiable on your picture and think about the exchange of value between you and them.

3. *Who shares your purpose and passion? Whilst many of the people you have identified can participate and add/receive value from your purpose, promise and proposition, the most effective way to connect is through what you and they have in common – particularly at the heart level – your passion and purpose.*

   Who in your picture shares your purpose and passion? Where do you and they fit well with regard to lifestyle, age, groups, networks, and interest? Look for shared ground with people and identify how your purpose and passion matches theirs. What is the exchange of value?

   Again, find a way to make these people clearly identifiable in your picture – in a way that is distinct from the people you identified in 2.

4. *There may be people you have yet to find who are missing from 2. And 3. They may be people you know you want to contact, or a person with specific skill/knowledge or a sponsor that you know you will need in order to fulfil on your purpose and proposition. Again, you may not know the people by name. It is fine to note it down as a role or function. Take a moment to add these people/capabilities to your picture.*

5. *Look at the people you have highlighted in 2. and 3. Sort them into three categories: critical to my purpose, promise and proposition; important; inform and stay in touch.*

You can now create a relationship map to represent your stakeholders as described in Addundum1, using the following zone definitions:

Zone A: the most critical and accessible stakeholders you already know who can support you with the realisation of your purpose, promise and proposition;

Zone B: accessible stakeholders who can introduce you to critical or important stakeholders you don't yet have access to;

Zone C: critical stakeholders you don't currently have access to but need to know in order to fulfil on your purpose, promise and proposition;

Zone D: stakeholders that you would love to meet but don't think you ever could;

Zone E: other important stakeholders who can support you; stakeholders you need to keep informed or stay in touch with but you can't yet see how they can assist you;

The people in Zone D are people who will massively accelerate and amplify the fulfilment of your purpose and delivery of your value proposition. In my experience just writing their names puts them in your consciousness and helps you see them – pretty much the same neural patterns that suddenly make you see lots of red Mercedes SLKs the moment you have bought yourself a red Mercedes SLK!

From Stakeholders to Advocates
Look through the 'critical and accessible stakeholders' and 'accessible stakeholders who can introduce you' on your stakeholder map and find your biggest advocates. I suggest that you start with them and ask them to introduce your message to other people who may be interested in your proposition.

As you look through your relationship map, find a way of visually identifying your biggest advocates.

Start with those you feel safe with. Let them (and yourself) know that it may not yet be perfect – it does not have to be. Use it to develop traction for what you have to offer. Involving them early engages them in what you are creating and gives them a sense that they are contributing to your future. This is something that most people love to do.

It is important to remember what your advocates care about and want to hear. Know that they found their way onto your relationship map because they share elements of your passion and purpose. They – as all human beings – care about success – theirs and yours. Success may look different for them, but nevertheless, they care about it. They are also your advocates, so you can be sure that they care about your success.

You may have concerns about engaging them in supporting your success. You may be concerned that it is bad to have a self-interest in approaching them. You may be concerned that they will say no and that it will impact your existing relationship in a negative way. Or you may have some other concern that would get in the way of you approaching them.

You must not forget that they are your advocates and they care about your success. Find ways to either share your concerns with them so that you can be sure it is not a problem for them. If not, look for other ways of letting your concerns go – perhaps by using some of the techniques in Chapter 6.

You are about to take your relationships with the 'advocates' you have identified up to a more committed level where you are there to support their wants and needs. Take time to understand and support them as well as share what you need from them.

If you are to contribute your full potential, you must experience yourself at 10/10. From here you can be at your current best, contribute your skills and knowledge, then grow yourself and others.

As you connect with your advocates, make sure that you keep your biggest advocates up to date with what you are up to (whilst not overdoing it and becoming a nuisance). Where they are critical stakeholders, ensure you send them emails with your latest news. Arrange regular coffee chats and share your successes with them – make sure you let them know how they have contributed to your success.

What you are looking to develop are quality connections. It is not about the number of people in your network.

Meeting and developing new advocates – increasing your support-base

As your current advocates introduce you to new people, a new set of concerns may arise. Again, you must find ways to manage/dissolve these concerns.

A few things to bear in mind:
- Keep in mind the importance of first impressions. Make sure you are at a 10/10 when you meet them. Do what you need to do to get yourself into a good space, where who you are and how you occur is consistent with your promise and proposition. Do

what you need to do to be at ease with yourself and others.
- When you meet potential new advocates, make sure to connect to them with your head, heart and gut.
- Be interested in what you can do for them, really get to know them. Be honest about your intention and contribution. Show up as your authentic self.

Useful techniques for managing yourself and your Fan Base as you get your message out there

The fine art of influencing through persuasion
Many women I meet resist proactively influencing for their own benefit and hence choose to let their work speak for itself. As our research shows however, it is clear that most organisations do not operate as pure meritocracies as the amount of data that would need to be assimilated in order to operate a pure meritocracy in large organisations makes it very difficult.

Perhaps this resistance to persuading is related to a reluctance to be seen as someone who is manipulative (a trait often ascribed to those I have identified in this book as 'fluffy') or coercive (a trait that is associated with our so called "alpha females") as opposed to being persuasive.

Let's address this by looking at some simple definitions of the four terms:

Influence: Affecting the development, behaviour or actions of another.

This can be achieved through:

1. **Persuasion**: Providing tangible value to others by having a conversation that accounts for their viewpoint.
2. **Manipulation**: Controlling or affecting cleverly or unscrupulously to further your own goals at the expense of others.

3. **Coercion**: Directing someone to do something using force or threats.

Someone who is being coercive is usually considered as aggressive: they stand up for their rights by violating the rights of others. They ignore the needs, wants and opinions of others in inappropriate ways. The "alpha female" is often said to demonstrate this behaviour – particularly when she is conflicted – either internally or externally.

Manipulation is often seen as submissive behaviour where someone fails to stand up for their rights and so gets disregarded by others. This person may communicate in apologetic or self-effacing ways. However, it is important to note that these submissive behaviours can often hide a level of passive aggression that gets demonstrated in hidden ways. If you exhibit behaviours that are typical of someone labelled as 'fluffy', your audience will experience passive aggression from you but often be unable to find evidence to support their experience. The impact will be on the level to which they trust and include you.

Persuasion employs assertive behaviour with the aim of a win-win outcome. Someone who is persuasive has self-worth. She respects the other person's rights, is in control of her feelings and actions and expresses herself honestly. It is not about proving yourself right at all costs, but rather about being taken seriously and having your opinions influence the decision making process.

Effective persuasion enables you to collaborate effectively by looking at the other person's perspective and having a conversation with them from a space of what is of benefit to them. This will enable you to engage your stakeholders, influence their opinions in a positive way because they experience that you have their interest at heart and seek to reach agreements that are in the interests of both parties.

In order to have a persuasive conversation, you listen authentically to the other person's viewpoint first. Listening authentically requires that you listen from the head, heart and gut (as described in addendum 1) and notice how they respond. This will enable you to understand their needs and wants and open up their listening to what you have to say. You can then speak about what you are looking to achieve – indicating the benefits of your approach and together you can explore alternatives. Don't forget that empathy and rapport are critical elements in all communications and are particularly important when you are having a conversation to persuade someone.

Prepare to Persuade
Making a persuasive case does require some preparation beforehand. Make sure you are clear on your own intentions for the conversation and what outcome you are looking to accomplish.

Think about the context that the person you are about to meet is in – reflect on what their objectives are, what is going on around them in terms of organisation, people they interact with, opportunities and threats they face and how the outcome you are looking for from the conversation can be a win/win for both of you.

You will need to have a clear proposal that communicates your promise and proposition, a reasoned argument that supports the logic of what you are proposing, evidence to support your logic and a full analysis of objections that might come up and how you would handle them. It is always a good idea to summarise your proposal at the beginning and end of your presentation of the proposal to ensure it is clear and heard.

Account for different styles
As a part of your preparation, think about the person you are about to meet and how they like to be communicated with. This will enable you to tailor your message so that it is presented in the best way for them to hear it.

For example, if you know beforehand that the person you are about to meet is an introvert who is quiet and introspective, make sure you give them time to think before you push them to speak - don't be ebullient and expressive and start to engage them in small talk before you get to the point – adjust your pace to theirs so that you can more easily connect with them. Give them time to reflect.

On the other hand, if you meet with an extrovert, they will be more comfortable with small talk and people who like social events. Make sure you don't lose their attention by going into minute detail. Keep it at the ideas level and at a faster pace that matches their propensity to move and think quickly.

Also think about whether they are task or people focused. Task focused people are highly committed to their work – they are irritated by interruptions and usually identify strongly with their organisation's aims. A good way for you to converse with them is to base what you say on facts and results. Don't push them about their feelings. Be business-like and formal.

However, know that this approach would not work as well with someone who is people focused. They prefer a cooperative approach to problem solving and want to develop a sense of empathy as they engage with you. These people like to be open, warm and are attentive listeners. A more informal style might work better with them.

When you have to Persuade without Authority
Very often you don't have authority over all the people you want to persuade or have as your advocates. They may not want to help you, or you may not have a good relationship with them. It may be that you are meeting someone for the first time and you have one opportunity to persuade them while you don't know them very well.

A model that I have found very effective in this situation is the Cohen Bradford Model illustrated in Fig 5. The Cohen Bradford model takes a six-stage approach to persuading someone based on a reciprocal approach.

Get your message out there – let your message be heard.
Time for another pause and reflect. Consider the different channels that are available for you to communicate your promise and proposition and which channels your stakeholders are most likely to use.

There are many to choose from: one to one/face to face meetings, email, mobile/telephone – voice and text, instant message, video calls, webinars, social media, online – internal and external, internal magazines and notice boards, internal and external networks, presentations to internal groups, expert bodies and the mass media to name but a few.

Think about your audience. A number of factors will determine which channels they use frequently including their age, their job type, their networks and their levels of technology adoption.

Identify which of these channels are best for communicating your promise and proposition to your stakeholder group and remember to factor in your competence in communicating through each channel. You will almost certainly want to use different channels for certain stakeholder groups or key individuals. You may want to develop skills in certain channels or start with the ones you know best. Alternatively, you may have someone in your virtual board who can do this for you – or perhaps someone in your network you can negotiate a value exchange with.

There is a volume of work to do in developing a deeper communication plan – for example, if you are going to build your profile through external networks or presenting papers at external conferences you will need to identify which of them will deliver the biggest impact for fulfilling on your purpose, promise and proposition.

Once you have chosen your mix of channels, you can start to prepare your message. Account for the fact that different channels require different types of messaging. Twitter will require short bursts of information whereas a presentation will require a lot of detail and thought. With communications such as conference papers, there will be a time lag as well. You will first have to submit an abstract or proposal. If your submission is accepted, you will then have to write a more detailed paper.

You can use your positioning statement as a starting point for developing tailored communications through each of these channels.

Your purpose here is to communicate who you are, your views and ideas to maximise your chances of people engaging you to deliver on your promise and your proposition.

Don't forget to review your communication plan with your virtual board before executing on it. Ask for their feedback on how well your message connects with them intellectually, emotionally and then inspire them to take action that will forward your opportunity to deliver on your promise and purpose. This will give you the best chance of success.

Part III

How it might go

Chapter 9 - Here's How Some of My Clients Did It

How to use this chapter
In this chapter, I share with you case studies from five of my clients at different stages in their career – the challenges they faced, how they resolved those challenges and what resulted from the work we did together.

It is designed to illustrate how women who are already successful have defined their purpose and fulfilled on their promise and proposition by applying some of the principles discussed in this book.

I am not recommending that you try to replicate what these women did as it may not work. The conversations I had with each of them were tailored to their circumstances and who they are. The transformations were caused more in the nature of the conversations than the specific actions they took. However, what you will get from reading these case studies is a sense of what can be achieved by applying some of the tools and techniques contained in this book to your situation. I hope you enjoy reading them.

As you might imagine, I am fierce about protecting the confidentiality of my clients, so be assured that each of these stories has their approval and I have altered a few details to make sure the stories cannot be traced.

Tina – Executive in a High Tech Firm

I met Tina at a networking lunch by the river in resplendent surroundings. We got to talking about her job and what her aspirations were. She had a background in political science and was working in the legal department for her firm at the time. Her accountability was to manage a set of issues in the legal and regulatory domain across markets for her company.

Shortly after this conversation, she engaged me as her coach.

In our first meeting, Tina told me that she wanted to be on the general management track, seeking an eventual C-suite role in her company.

Now Tina was in her late twenties and clearly successful and ambitious. To someone looking at her from the outside, they would definitely put her in the Alpha Female category, thinly veiled with a gentle manner about her.

My first question to her was – what about marriage and family?

This might seem like an odd question for an Executive Coach to ask her client at their first meeting. However, I have come across many women who have taken an ambitious career trajectory without thinking about their overall life plan. The result has been an unexpected derailment when they have children and their career stalls.

Tina had not had much luck in the love department and was not particularly committed to finding a relationship. If it happened, that would be good, but was not something she was going to focus on.

So we got to work on what was important to her. We started with her values using a timeline based approach to surface what values were being fulfilled by her happiest moments and what values were not being fulfilled during her darkest moments in her life so far.

What was interesting to me was that as she spoke, and as we got to know one another, the person I was seeing was not at all the alpha female that is initially presented. Here was a woman who wanted a garden and warm home, family time and to travel. She wanted to contribute and inspire people. If she had a partner, she would want someone to share all this with, but it would have to be someone who also supported her ambitions in life.

We then explored her deepest fears – being selfish showed up as a fear.

The guilt of not being around enough for the people she loved or for giving enough time to her work, over planning and sub-par delivery all featured on her list of deepest fears.

After that meeting Tina took on creating some vision board collages for us to explore when we next met. This provided a rich focus for our discussion on her vision and purpose and she became clear that in order to achieve her purpose she would have to broaden her experience to include P&L, direct business development and commercial competencies. Tina took on finding a secondment position to develop these critical skills in addition to her day job.

At our next meeting Tina started to complain about a male colleague in her department who seemed to be favoured by her female up-line despite Tina working harder and producing better results on specific projects. She felt that she often did most of the work to ensure that deliverables were produced and deadlines met, but did not get the recognition for it – whereas her male colleague Henry would not deliver on his part of the piece of work leaving her to pick up the pieces to make sure that the team met their commitments. She felt very frustrated by this situation.

So how did Henry end up having a more productive relationship and more acknowledgements from the up-line Christina?

Through our conversation, Tina discovered that her 'assertive' style where she was often communicating to Christina about how she had 'saved the day' showed her up as aggressive – referred to as 'alpha female' in this book, and that Henry was just more laid back and had a tendency to focus on what would have the biggest impact for the team rather than get side-tracked by 'good' ideas.

Tina started to work on her automatic need to prove herself although she continued to work hard. She could see that her options in her current team were limited and that she would be better off developing relationships in the unit to which she was seconded. However, her loyalty to Christina (who had been a great mentor and sponsor for her in the past) meant that she kept doing a great job in her 'day job' as well – so effectively doing two jobs.

Tina was doing very well in her secondment – learning a lot about the commercials of product development and marketing. She was building a great relationship with Melissa who ran this Division. So much so that a position at a higher level was about to be advertised and Melissa said she would like Tina to apply for it.

Tina was very excited about this and could not contain herself when we next met.

She already had a meeting scheduled with Melissa's main internal client Mark whom she had met in a previous leadership interaction. Tina was keen to demonstrate to Mark her experience and why she would be a good fit for the team.

We discussed her outcomes and how to be with Mark so that she created a good impression. Unfortunately, the feedback on this meeting from Melissa regarding her meeting with Mark was not great. Mark thought Tina was only interested in the role for what it could do for her and not in what was good for the team. He saw her as too ambitious. She did get to interview for the position but the role went to another hire.

Tina was really starting to see in a stark way how in moments of stress – or when she felt she was being treated unfairly that her sharp side would come out and her values were often compromised.

Listening to Tina I noticed a repeating pattern around her behaviour.

When I first challenged Tina about this, she could not see it, so we did some script work. Her script with these colleagues was essentially that the individuals she struggled with she considered to not work as hard as her or were unreliable and often tried to exclude her.

We tracked back through Tina's life to explore where this script was formed and identified several points in her life through which the script evolved, including very personal moments throughout her childhood, university years and in her first set of jobs. These moments involved small stories with friends, especially in the challenging years of adolescence. We also spoke about Tina's family, and understood how she always wanted to prove herself, regardless of gender, regardless of the challenge ahead.

We started to draw connections between all these stories and understand how she then developed the kind of characteristics of an 'alpha female' in order to prove people wrong about not being able to achieve things that were reserved for traditional male roles.

The interesting significance here is that this script had led her to great success to date, however, it is a script she had no control over. It crept in automatically.

So in certain circumstances, she would appear as overly aggressive and self-obsessed. Having seen that this script was just something she had invented to survive the perceptions of others especially in regard to roles women could play in the workforce, or in life generally, she was able to take ownership of it. She could run that part of her 'programming' when she chose to, but she could also write new scripts that gave her freedom to behave differently when required. It was as if all those 'bags of coal' that she had been carrying on her back based on each of the foregoing scripts she had added to her belief system over time could finally be let go and she was free to be herself again. She could now write a new script for herself – keeping those behaviours she wants to keep and letting go of those that were no longer of use or in the way of her progress. She could also rewrite this script whenever it was no longer useful.

We used the analogy of software programming to examine this. Up until this point, Tina was smart enough to know that certain behaviours did not work and so was trying to debug and reprogramme those behaviours. However, this just made for an inefficient and sometimes ineffective programme. She saw that now she was aware of the old programme, she could actually delete it and write a whole new programme that encapsulated the best of her past behaviours and add in routines that would give her freedom from the old script.

The new script she created included these statements:
1. I am curious about solving problems.
2. I listen and enable others to achieve their goals.
3. I can let go, scale and trust others.

She started to pay more attention to her daily communication and to her approach to teamwork.

She began reflecting on what she really wants. Her purpose in life – which she articulated in a way that included connecting others and creating great products, helped her reflect on the present and future.

It is no surprise that she became a bit more chilled out through this process and started dating.

Soon after this, Melissa – who continued to be impressed by Tina's ability throughout her secondment shared that her Division would be growing and that some transfers at the same level would become available soon.

This time Tina really took the time to think about the whole team – how she could add value, what the various stakeholders in Melissa's team would care about and what kind of value exchange would make the transition work to enable everyone to achieve on their goals.

She transferred a few months later and was careful to ensure that her accountabilities in her previous position were handed over immaculately whilst at the same time taking time to get to know the people in her new team – a little less time on the task and a bit more time on the people.

At the time of writing, her team has already expanded and there are openings for achieving the next level in her career. She continues to develop herself in getting the best out of different types of people – sales staff, engineers, finance people and creatives.

Oh and on the personal front, she is in an inspiring and happy relationship with her partner and they are creating an adventurous future together.

Rebecca – Director in a large public utility

Rebecca had a successful change management career in the city and then moved to a large public utility doing a similar kind of job so that she could have a more balanced lifestyle with less travel than she believed was possible in the commercial sector.

The company she moved to was very male dominated and technically based.

Rebecca was more of a generalist and delivered high quality work in the change management space prior to taking up a role in HR. Her job in HR was quite removed from the company frontline and she was concerned about how she could be more visible in a male dominated environment whilst working in an HR business support role.

We started by exploring Rebecca's Professional Brand – her values, purpose, promise and proposition. Through this, she clarified what was important to her and what she had to offer.

We then explored her communications strategy and selected a virtual board and stakeholders for her to start contacting.

In parallel, we looked at challenges that came up during the course of our work together.

Rebecca was very focused, and when she was being focused on completing a report her immediate reaction to spontaneous approaches from her team landed as abrupt and annoyed.

This was not Rebecca's intention at all. She had told her team that they could approach her when they needed and really wanted to be available for them.

For her team, her words and actions did not match what she had told them about being available especially when she was under pressure.

This meant that her team was not authentically experiencing the consistency and constancy of her Professional Brand.

When she realised this, she was able to check her own behaviours, but also communicate to the team that her behaviour in that situation was just that she was focused and it took her a few minutes to take her attention away from the work at hand to be able to be with them.

They agreed some basic ways of working that resulted in her team experiencing her as available whilst still having time to focus on deadline driven thought pieces when she had to. One example was her highlighting time in her diary for when she was available for them and asking her PA to manage these slots to ensure that people had access to her.

Through the Professional Branding conversations, I could see that Rebecca was someone who liked to have it all handled and where she thought something was not going to get delivered, she would take it on herself. This led to a lot of stress for her – and her teams felt disempowered. We discussed this and factored it into her communications plan.

As a part of her communications strategy to her team, Rebecca started having 'Town Hall' meetings with her team. However, these were Town Halls with a difference. Rebecca took on being open and shared her weaknesses and challenges as well as her strengths in these meetings. She did this not from a place of inferiority, but from a place of strength. This opened up a space for her team to be open and honest with her and many potential problems got identified and resolved early. This was a risky strategy for Rebecca, but handled properly it made a big difference for her. She was able to turn around a couple of dysfunctional teams she inherited to start working as a tight team and deliver quality work way ahead of deadlines.

Another key part of her communications plan was to develop awareness of who she was and what she had to offer (her promise and proposition) with senior managing directors in the organisation so that she, her contribution and her proposition could be 'known' by key decision makers. This was a critical element for her to achieve her next promotion.

Rebecca really struggled with this. Her job did not naturally give her access to these people and she was reluctant to attend meetings unless she had something of value to add. She was also not willing to network in order to build the relationships that would give her access.

As if by magic, an opportunity opened up for her.

Her colleague whose accountability was to act as a client manager to this MD community took a sideways move, leaving the perfect vacancy for her.

She found out about the vacancy on a Friday morning. She knew she wanted the role, but also knew she needed a little more time in her current role in order to finish the job she had started.

She pondered on it all of Friday and on her way home sent a text to her up line expressing her interest in the role.

To her surprise, she got a reply to her text on the Sunday asking her to pop in for a chat on Monday.

Rebecca was expecting that there would be a whole cumbersome interview process and in her mind did not think her manager would want her to move given the needs of her current role. So imagine her surprise when her manager said she could have the job – and started to discuss the migration path.

Rebecca started in her new role a month later and is thoroughly enjoying her work with the MD community. Her natural talent with people, her commitment to excellent delivery and providing what her internal clients want – combined with her broader change management and HR knowledge makes her an instant hit.

Not everyone will have this kind of luck although (as you will have read earlier in this book) I believe that Rebecca caused this for herself by setting her mind on what was next for her.

Alisa – Managing Director, Architects Firm

Alisa had spent the last 10 years building an international architects firm. She was dealing with the challenge of succession.

Whilst she had built a robust and capable team when it came to delivering projects, it always fell to her to sell the work in and manage the clients.

She considered merging her company with another firm, but was concerned that she would then lose control of her brand and that her business would go downhill.

She also wondered why she kept getting turned down for so many contracts when she knew her competition entries were so much better. Her conclusion was that 'this is a male dominated industry and that's just how it is'.

Also, her parents were aging and as an only child, she wanted to spend more time with them as they grew older.

All these challenges left her confused about what she should do and which direction she should go in.

She joined one of our 9-month programmes that took place in a luxury spa because she saw it as an opportunity to give herself some 'me time' and reflect on what the next 30 years of her life would look like.

Having created her vision, purpose and the third chapter of her life, she realised that what was really missing for her was recognition of her life's work and contribution to architecture.

Having looked at various options for having this recognition, she chose to enter herself for a major award. She did not honestly expect to get shortlisted as some high profile architects had also entered. She went through the gruelling process of writing up the application, getting testimonials (which were actually rewards in themselves), being shortlisted and attending a short but thorough interview – where she was up against eminent architects who had worked on some of the world's largest building projects.

Imagine her surprise when she actually won the award!

She had opportunities to speak about her life's work to a large audience during the awards ceremony and then again at the organiser's annual conference.

She finally felt fully acknowledged for the amazing spaces that her company had built around the world.

She could now put her hat down and relax.

She sold her business to another local company and plans to work on more community based projects and spend more time with her parents.

I include Alisa's story here to demonstrate that it is not always about reaching for the stars. Sometimes, when you look deep into your authentic purpose and the future you want for yourself, you may find that actually, you don't want to work anymore. Alisa is looking forward to a more leisurely pace where she will enjoy the third chapter of her life, knowing that her team have a solid future and good prospects, and she can turn her attention to specific other interests she wants to follow up.

Jennifer – Senior Manager, International Retailer

Jennifer was upset because she had been passed over for promotion twice within 3 years. The first time, she thought she had a good relationship with her manager and so was surprised that in a re-organisation, someone she had recruited to work with her got the promotion instead. She then felt that she did not fit in to her organisation - that her interests in the arts and her more gentle ways were not valued.

After this, she felt that she always had so much to do, and whilst she generally got everything done, she was on the edge of dropping the ball. She now had another person between her and her former manager.

Her nature was not to push her way forward but rather to focus on being loyal to the company brand and do a good job that contributed value. She demonstrated some classic 'fluffy' behaviours – particularly not speaking up and then resenting it.

A few years later, there was another vacancy at the next level up that she could have been considered for.

She was convinced that she would not get it and waited for the person who was now her second up-line to tell her she would not be considered for the role.

We started our coaching conversations around this time.

We explored her situation and her environment.

We looked at what was important to her.

She seemed to me to be somewhat resigned about her situation and very angry – although she would not communicate her anger openly.

We worked together to 'get under' the anger. To really give her a way to express the anger and reflect on where it had begun.

Jennifer traced it back to a school experience where she had been put in a difficult situation regarding her 11+ where she was just thrown in to it without any support or training. She did not get the school she wanted and ended up in an average school.

She felt let down and resentful.

This same pattern was repeating every time she didn't get chosen for a promotion.

In our conversations, she realised that in each instance, she had not actually put herself forward. She had waited to be chosen – just as she had waited to be helped in her 11+.

She was then able to have a conversation with her manager; taking responsibility for the situation she found herself in and making clear requests of him about what she did really want. She realised that she did not actually want the jobs she would have been promoted to.

Instead, she created for herself an EMEA wide job in which she could work on something she was passionate about – the diversity and inclusion agenda across the non-US part of the business.

In this process, she also got to stop feeling that she did not fit in. She realised (as in the diversity and inclusion business case that is widely accepted today), that her gentle manner and less self-focused way of operating at work actually brought immense value in terms of rich thought, consideration and being able to deal with a much broader range of challenges. She was able to 'own fluffy' in a way that actually gave her a bit of an edge whilst still being very much herself. She accepted that she did not have to develop more aggressive 'alpha female' qualities in order to progress.

Jennifer has gone on to implement a number of leading edge initiatives for her organisation and is recognised as a pioneer in causing the required culture change there.

Justine – From UK to Global Head of Compensation whilst becoming a mother of two

Justine was 7 months pregnant when she had a conversation with me about her concerns. She had already done very well in her career to date and was worried about how having her baby would impact her career.

Should she dedicate her time to being a full time mother? Should she come back to work very quickly so that she could continue her career trajectory?

What would people be saying about her now that she was about to become a mother? Would she still be given the same kinds of opportunities?

Justine asked to work with me on our maternity coaching package.

We started by exploring what was important to her – and actually acknowledging that she could not know at this time what would happen once that bundle of joy was in her arms. We both knew of many mothers who had left on maternity leave fully planning to come back as soon as possible and then realised that actually what was most important to them was to be a great mother – as well as others who had planned to take a full year out and then returned within 6 weeks because they missed their work so much.

Justine's motivational map shed light on where she was likely to go, but we put that into the background as she did not want to make any decisions before the baby was born.

We discussed a broad range of parameters together – including the implications for her and her husband and their careers, the pros and cons from her perspective of different child care options, how much to have parents involved, their living situation and many other things that were important to her.

In our last conversation before her baby was born, we focused on letting go. Leaving all that was connected with the world of work behind so that she could create a space to just be a mother for a few months.

By this time, she had a pretty good idea that she would want to return to work after her maternity leave but left the final choice to be made after baby arrived.

Justine was well prepared when she had her baby. She had thought through everything in a very clear way and had a broad range of options to support her decision-making.

She took a full year out to enjoy her time with Louise and do everything a full time mother would do.

Once back at work, Justine made a well-defined separation between work and home. When she was at work, she was there 100%, delivered excellent work and made sure she put work first. She had after all put everything in place to ensure that Louise was well looked after with a full-time nanny who had been working with her for the last 3 months of maternity leave and hence did everything just as Justine wanted.

The quality of Justine's contribution and her active management of stakeholders was rewarded with a promotion to European Head of Compensation.

During her first year back Justine found herself pregnant with baby 2.

This time it was less stressful and she took just 9 months out to be with Louise and Jed. During this time she loved being a mum and created deep relationships with her two babies. Having the Nanny there meant that her mind was free to take a more relaxed approach and really enjoy this time with her children.

Interestingly, Justine had continued to produce good work and develop her stakeholder network such that one month after returning she was asked to take on the role of global head of compensation.

For me, Justine's story is very inspiring. I admire the way she took charge of her future, accepted that in truth she could not be a super mum at the same time as fulfilling her potential at work. She made clear choices and went for it.

It may appear that 'it was alright for her' because she could afford a full time nanny. However, this was far from the truth at the beginning. She just chose what was right for her and her family and although money was tight. They had to make significant sacrifices after the first baby, but she stood by her chosen path and realised her potential. Watch this space – because my view is that Justine has only just begun her career trajectory.

Chapter 10 – What Made It Work for Them and How You Can Do the Same

1. They reached out and took action

As you will have seen with each of the women featured in Chapter 9, they moved themselves from being at the effect of their circumstances to cause their future and make clear choices.

Some of you may be able to read this book and do that for yourself using the tools and techniques contained here.

For others, you may want to find someone you trust, who really understands you and will be your champion to make sure you achieve what you want and coach you through the hard times. If you choose this option, please make sure you give them full permission to challenge you – especially when you don't want to take the required actions. Know that you have chosen them because you fully trust them and their whole interest in challenging you is to support you in getting what you want – even when you don't want to because you are either too confronted or too scared.

If you are committed to realising your full value, it is now time for you to own that journey and invest in you.

2. They dealt with what was in the way

They learned to be compassionate with their inner Diva, acknowledging her voice and speaking to her with confidence and credibility so that they could go to work on causing their futures.

They handle the shrinkers around them in a similar way – whether they were at work, in their family or community.

They made sure that their level of presence matched their purpose, promise and proposition – whether that was in their physical presence (dress, voice, stance, accessories) or their internal conversations and self-belief.

They allowed others to contribute value – they developed relationships and an emotional connection with each of their virtual board members and let those people be excited by what they were up to.

3. They committed to an authentic purpose and kept that in front of them

It took courage for them to reach out and engage a complete stranger to assist them. They knew they wanted to achieve something, but could not see the wood from the trees.

The first thing they had to be willing to do was clear out the debris and clutter from their past. They identified any scripts that may have been useful in the past but were now stopping them in certain situations. They sifted and sorted and selected what they wanted to keep; then erased the scripts they had lived their lives by up to that point that no longer served them. They then wrote a new script that included the elements they wanted to keep from the past as well as new, more empowering scripts to take them forward to fulfil on their purpose. They practiced spotting the disempowering situations and embedding the new scripts into their behaviours.

They identified the diamond within them and let it shine in a way that reflected their authentic personality. They identified what was important to them and what they are good at. They created a clear purpose for their future and focused on that. They learned to have compassion for themselves and took pride in who they are.

They learned to communicate fully – from their head, heart and gut – in a way that was congruent with who they are.

Once they had created their new vision, purpose, promise and proposition, they chose it powerfully and managed to stick to it – letting go of guilt each time it came up – for come up it did.

4. They reached deep within – even when they did not want to.

When things did not go their way, they looked at themselves – not others. They really owned the realisation of the future they had chosen. They became leaders in their own lives. If you think about it, this makes a lot of sense. You can't actually do much about another person's behaviour or actions, but you can take responsibility for your own…and when you do that, the other person often gets to see your point of view because they have had the rare experience of being truly heard and respected.

They listened to conversations that they really did not want to hear – whether that was with me challenging them or with their colleagues and family. For some of them, their family or colleagues were critical or had concerns that they were being too ambitious. They also listened to some conversations where they had to accept acknowledgement and appreciation and their family and colleague's belief that they absolutely could do it – even if their negative 'Diva' told them they couldn't the moment things got a bit tough.

5. They showed who they are and what they stand for with clarity, consistency and constancy

They did what they had to do to demonstrate the clarity, consistency and constancy of their proposition as well as tangible performance over time so that people believed they would deliver – even in crisis situations.

To do this, they had to work on how they presented themselves in person, online and even when they were out and about for personal activities such as shopping or going to the movies with their partner.

They stuck to the choices they had made about their purpose – not giving themselves permission to be a 'purpose butterfly'.

They let themselves rise out from the crowd and be known as the best – using social proof such as presenting papers, using social media and winning awards.

In summary, they took ownership for their futures – using whatever government schemes and employer initiatives were available to support their progression – but they did not wait for any other agency to do it for them. They OWNED IT and WON.

Like them, I hope this book enables you to find *Authentic You* and fulfil on your purpose and what is important to you.

ADDENDA

Addendum 1 – Your Inner Power Toolkit

Power Tool 1: Deep listening – using your head, heart and gut.

Mostly in corporate life we use our head, suppressing our heart and gut. This has a massive impact on human beings – particularly women.

Here is a brief guide to how you can connect with your head, heart and gut.

The ability to connect from the head, heart and gut is particularly relevant in enabling people to feel that you are listening deeply to what they are saying and have the experience of being fully heard. This is a rare and valuable art to cultivate.

Let's start by looking at what it is not:
— It is not pseudo-listening where you are pretending to listen but pre-occupied by other thoughts.
— It is not point scoring – where you are listening for how you can show you are better than them.
— It is not rehearsing – where you are thinking about and planning what you are going to say next.
— It is not cherry picking – where you are hearing only what you want to hear and discarding the rest.
— It is not filling gaps – where you interrupt the other person while they are taking a moment to reflect before continuing.
— It is not side stepping – where you brush over the other's emotions using clichés and cold statements.

So then, how do you listen from your head, heart and gut?

When you are listening from you head, heart and gut, you engage authentically with the person and what they are saying. Be genuinely interested in them and what they have to say. You can use questions to clarify anything you don't understand and also to demonstrate that you are engaging with what they are saying.

Often, there will be something that you also want to communicate, so don't forget your proposal to them and what you are intending as an outcome from the conversation. Keep the conversation focused and bring it back if it goes off target. As always, bring empathy and rapport, remembering to manage your emotions by bringing yourself back to your intended outcome, what you value about them, how they are showing up for you and why you have chosen them for this particular conversation.

A good way to practice and develop your ability to connect with your head heart and gut is to find a reflective space, close your eyes and look at your head from the backs of your eyes. Then ask your head the question. Once you have an answer, write that down. Close your eyes again, put your hand on your heart and ask your heart. Write down what you heart says. Finally, put your hand on your solar plexus – the space just below your rib cage at the top of your tummy and do the same. As you get more practiced at connecting with your head heart and gut, you will be able to go through this process more quickly and eventually it will become automatic.

Power Tool 2: References to the reality of energetics
Scientists like Dr. Konstantin Korotkov, of St Peters-burg State Technical University who uses techniques such as

bio-electrophotography to study energy fields and consequent outcomes; The Princeton Engineering Anomalies Research (PEAR) Laboratory that is studying and demonstrating how the human mind and intention has a subtle capacity to influence the output of devices called 'random event generators' through applied experiments that look at how the human mind can influence (for example) the 50/50 balance of a coin tossing experiments; in addition to psychologists like Professor Barbara L. Fredrickson who have studied the human energy field and how it can affect mental and physical health. Quantum science is now being used to further explain how the energy field (that in the spiritual world is sometimes called the 'aura') can intend and create desired outcomes at a sub-conscious level.

Power Tool 3: What is a Breakthrough Goal?
Start from the premise that there are four kinds of goals that you can set yourself:
1. Business as Usual: this is not really a goal. It is more about continuing the status quo and expecting to produce the same level of results or better.
2. Stretch Goals: these goals are ambitious however, I am fairly confident that I can accomplish them. To achieve them will require me to work harder and become more efficient as well as take on some level of innovation and creativity.
3. Breakthrough Goals: these goals are beyond stretch goals and the goals that I aim to set myself. I know deep down that they can be attained, but cannot see how yet. They give me butterflies in my stomach when I imagine these goals being realised. I feel a bit on edge and nervous about whether I can really do it.

4. Dream/Pie in the Sky: I think it is essential to have dream goals. They nurture me and give me something to look forward to. However, they are not the kind of goals that could be achieved within the year – and definitely not something a sponsor or partner would take seriously if I told them I would accomplish them within a year.

To achieve a breakthrough goal, you have to go beyond what you know already. You have to think in new and creative ways. This in itself is of value, however the most valuable aspect of having a breakthrough goal is that it causes you to address those challenges that have kept you stuck for years because you 'don't know how to.'

Power Tool 4: Business Plan on a Page
A good plan is a valuable tool for making sure that you are on course. It does not need to be complex. Here's how to design a basic plan that is easy for you and your virtual board to understand and from which to manage your development and fulfilment.

You can take each one-year breakthrough goal and apply the business plan on a page format to it.

Once you have identified your breakthrough goals, the next step is to identify the areas of your work and non-work life that are involved in delivering the goals. Examples of possible areas are: stakeholders, sales, P&L, team, time, family. Which areas of your business and your life do you need to pay attention to in order to deliver the breakthrough goal you are creating a plan for? I recommend that you focus on the 5 most important areas that have to be managed in order to deliver the goal.

Once you have identified the 5 areas, start from the last quarter and for each area identify what milestones have to be reached in order to achieve the goal. Once you have identified milestones for quarter 4, you can move back to quarter 3 and identify the milestones that have to be achieved by the end of quarter 3 in order for you to deliver your quarter 4 milestones. You will find this process challenging and want to start at quarter 1. My recommendation is that you bear with the pain and work backwards. Working backwards calls for breakthrough thinking – it breaks our linear patterns. This is the thinking that is required to deliver a breakthrough goal. If you start thinking in a linear way, starting at quarter 1, you will most likely deliver a stretch goal result at best.

Finally, you can use the business plan on a page format as illustrated in Fig 3. to create a visual plan that will enable you to track progress.

I often begin each quarter with a similar plan for that quarter – breaking the timelines up to every two weeks in order to ensure I achieve the quarterly goals.

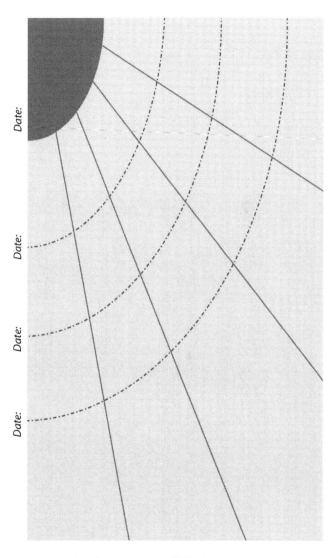

FIG 3. Plan on a Page – AKA The Sun Ray Diagram

Power Tool 5: Relationship Map Guide
A relationship map can be useful in supporting you as you manage the relationships with your stakeholders, target audience and virtual board.

At the centre of the relationship map is you. As you move from Zone A to Zone C, the people on the map become less important and urgent for your purpose. You could also add further zones if you have more than 3 categories of stakeholder.

For example, with the stakeholder mapping exercise in Chapter 8, the zones would be defined as follow:

Zone A: the most critical and accessible stakeholders you already know who can support you with the realisation of your purpose, promise and proposition;

Zone B: accessible stakeholders who can introduce you to critical or important stakeholders you don't yet have access to;

Zone C: critical stakeholders you don't currently have access to but need to know in order to fulfil on your purpose, promise and proposition;

Zone D: other important stakeholders who can support you; stakeholders you need to keep informed or stay in touch with but you can't yet see how they can assist you;

If you want to use the relationship map for your Virtual Board, you can populate the map as follows: In zone A identify the people who are critical now to fulfilling on this year's goals and for your long-term future. Also place here virtual board potentials from the people on your list that you already have good relationships with. You can think about how these people can be introducers to your Zone B team. In Zone B place people who are important but you may not have good relationships with yet. Mark the critical ones with a red star. These are the people you need to get to through your introducers. In Zone C, place people who could become important in the future but are not critical at this time. Outside Zone C, place people you know who may not be on your virtual board, but are influencers to Board members and other potential stakeholders.

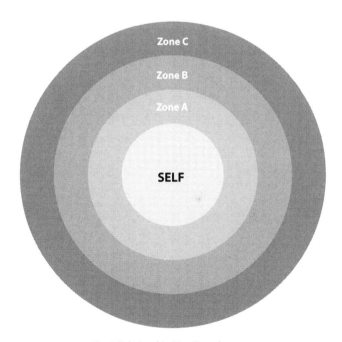

Fig 4. Relationship Map Template

Power Tool 6: Techniques for managing your 'Self-Talk'

As you will know by now, self-talk can spiral into disempowerment and become a major barrier to your progress. Here I guide you through a number of techniques that will support people in dealing with negative self-talk.

Bit 1: Scripts

In Chapter 6, I discussed Eric Berne's script identification process in some level of detail when it comes to looking at your past and how it stops you.

The script method is just as useful when it comes to self-talk that gets in the way in the present moment.

Whenever you catch yourself being stuck – or talking negatively to yourself, take a look at what is happening, what meaning you are making of it, how it makes you feel and what action you are drawn to take. Look at whether that action is going to have a positive of negative impact on your passion and purpose. Pause and write a new script.

Bit 2: Reframe

Reframing your thoughts and your communication is a quick and impactful way to deal with your self-talk. For example:

— 'self-promotion is not a good quality'
  Reframe: 'It is my job to let people know what I am doing. It will avoid duplication and allow best practice to spread, being of benefit to my team and the business as a whole.'

— 'Managing Profile is selfish and vain.'

Reframe: 'Managing profile is an integral part of every social interaction.'

- 'I am at a disadvantage because I am the only woman in my department.
Reframe: 'Being the only woman in my team means that people will remember what I say and do so it is a great opportunity to be noticed.

- 'I don't have enough time to do more than my job at work. Networking is a luxury.
Reframe: 'networking is an important part of my job – and I make time to do what is important.'

- 'I believe it is selfish to invest in my own development'
Reframe: 'I am not able to be at my best if I don't invest in my development.'

- 'I don't like playing politics'
Reframe: 'Politics is just social interaction. I need to know what's going on in the wider ecosystem of my organisation and industry so that my work is relevant.'

Bit 3: Mindfulness

Mindfulness is a practice originating from the practices and teaching of Gautama Buddha over 2500 years ago. It develops the capacity to pay attention in a particular way based on increasing the quality of present moment awareness with purpose and in a non-judgemental way. It is more about a way of being than a way of doing.

Through mindfulness you will develop a capacity to choose how you deploy your attention and manage the wandering mind.

A simple definition of Mindfulness is provided by Mindfulness expert Michael Chaskalson, where he identifies the two core dimensions of mindfulness as:

1. Wisdom – the ability to allow what is the case to be the case...not how is 'should or should not be.' Wisdom by this definition is to accept reality as it is and embrace what's going on. This enables you to choose what is – just as it is – without judgement.
2. Compassion – being compassionate enables us to still our inner critical voice. Having compassion for yourself enables you to deal with self-talk such as 'I'm not good enough'. Through mindfulness, you access an ability to be 'enough' – not too much or too little. This develops a way to deal with what history has delivered with gentleness and kindness towards yourself and others.

To develop strength in mindfulness you have to pay attention to the impact of what triggers your 'self-talk' on all five senses. This practice will enable your 'self-talk' to subside. The first step is to notice it and just let it be.

Training your mental processes in this way - with wisdom and compassion – will leave you in a place to make a choice free from judgements and triggers. It will move you from 'automaticity' which is the state we mostly operate in – and which supports us in our day to day lives to get things done without using up too much brain-power, to developing an ability to be in the moment when we choose to. The downside of automaticity is that we may miss important signals such as eye movements, gestures and tone of voice. Some of what we have automated can sometimes get in our way. A prime example of this is self-talk designed to protect us from scary or threatening situations – such as 'I'm not good enough, so I will leave it this time', or 'I am not ready yet – I need more training.'

Using a mindfulness practice – such as bringing attention to the impact on the five senses – you can step out of such limiting automatic thoughts, consider the facts and make a real choice.

Meditation and reflective inquiry such as the reflective inquiry exercises contained in this book will also help develop your ability to expand your mindfulness capacity.

To move the practice of mindfulness from the theoretical to the applied, here is an example taken from my dissertation journal of when I managed to shift state by bringing mindfulness to the situation:

September 19th: I have been exploring 'mindfulness'. What I see is that when I believe someone is just letting me be – being compassionate and non-judgmental with me, then I give myself permission to give of my fullest and be fully open. When I don't have that sense, I am more reserved and cautious, resulting in conversations that range from 'reasonable' to 'unrecoverable.'

I am now exploring the conversation that I bring mindfulness - wisdom and compassion - to a situation rather than wait for someone else to provide the right environment for me to shine. I have been practicing with that around my family today. Particularly with my Dad who I sometimes feel I have to tread on eggshells around or start a conversation that is of interest to him but that will not result in us getting into an argument. I started out by practicing 'wisdom' – just allowing my Dad to be my Dad. I noticed increased peace of mind, however, I was still trying to think of an interesting conversation to start up. I was wondering why that was and realised that actually, I was not allowing me to be me (wisdom dimension). This was a Eureka moment for me. I NEVER JUST LET MYSELF BE! In that moment, I started to have compassion for myself and just let myself, my Dad and the situation 'be' as it is – not how I thought it should be. I could feel my body relax. I was present to how much I loved my Dad and I just stayed still – appreciating who he is for me and appreciating myself as a generous human being. The outcome of letting myself just be and not having to be a certain way in order to come up with a certain result is that we had a joyful and meaningful conversation over lunch where we could speak with one another without my having angst and him getting irritated/argumentative.

Mindfulness is also said (as defined by Shapiro and Carlson) to have three core elements: intention (knowing why you are paying attention through reflection), attention (attending to your experience in the present moment) and attitude (being accepting, curious and open-hearted) – that connect with each other in interconnected ways. Whilst this provides a strong theoretical framework, I believe that Chaskalson's concepts of wisdom and compassion capture the essence of mindfulness and provide an easily applied, practical definition that you can use day to day.

Mindfulness – as with all the managing self-talk tools I guide you through here, is a massive topic, but just being aware of and practicing the two dimensions of wisdom and compassion will take you a long way towards mastering your self-talk.

Bit 4: Reprogramming Technique: Use Anchors to change states
This technique is taken from the now popular NLP approach to dealing with unhelpful 'Self-Talk.' It locks in a positive experience that you can access whenever you feel disempowered.

Imagine a situation when you performed at your best and everything thing seems to flow. Reach back and feel the emotion that existed in your body in that moment and what sensory experiences you had in different parts of your body. Let yourself experience those feelings and experiences again.

Keeping that emotional state in mind, find an anchor that locks that state in for you. An anchor is usually a physical action – such as putting pressure on a certain part of your hand or reciting a mantra that brings back those sensations. Associating the state of performance and the emotions you felt then with a physical action will support you to move to a more empowering state. In this state you will be able to listen from what the other person is actually dealing with.

Whenever you find yourself in a stressful situation, (for example, if you are depending on someone to produce a deliverable by a certain deadline for a critical project and they say they don't have enough time), activate the anchor until you experience a state change. Once you have done this, you will be able to have a more productive conversation. At first it may take a long time to activate the anchor and change state, but with practice it will become as easy as flicking a switch.

Before starting the conversation, remind yourself that you are responsible for everything that occurs around you and that you have everything you need to be a powerful person.

By doing this you will be able to forgive yourself and others for whatever is upsetting you about their actions, communications and behaviour.

You will then be able to have a conversation to understand what they are dealing with. They will feel acknowledged and understood such that they will listen to what you have to say and where you are coming from. From here you can have a conversation to achieve what you both are looking to achieve without the negative energy that comes with conflict.

Bit 5: Meditative Technique: Ho-o-pono-pono
A good friend of mine, Almira Ross taught me the following Hawaiian technique known as '*ho-o-pono-pono*' This is an ancient practice for forgiveness and reconciliation. The technique uses a mantra to free oneself from staying stuck in anger and frustration. The Mantra follows this sequence: "I am sorry, please forgive me, I love you and I thank you", blended with breathing and meditation to release the tensions that get in the way of clear communication. Here is how to practice ho-o-pono-pono:

Ask yourself: "what is it in me that is causing this situation?" This requires you taking all the blame away from others and own that you are causing the situation to persist. If you can't do this, then do not use this technique as it won't work.

The *ho-o-pono-pono* Mantra:
1. Acknowledge the source of life as that exists for you for its unconditional love. It may be a creator, other

spiritual source or where you believe life comes from. I will call it here the universal source.
2. Say "I am sorry" – here you are taking responsibility for the situation and for any negative manifestation you experience so that you can create a space for healing. You are not directing this apology at anyone in particular, you are saying that you are sorry for whatever it is you have done to cause the situation. Reflect on what that is.
3. Say "Please forgive me", asking for forgiveness from the universal source for any opinions of negative thoughts that have contributed to this situation. You must do this knowing that forgiveness is already granted – because it is in your power to do that.
4. Say "I love you" to the universal source. Love is the healing power. This, if said authentically will generate an immediate feeling of well-being. It will tune your mind to a more peaceful space.
5. Say "I thank you" to acknowledge that your situation has been heard by the universal source and that source has now freed you up to move forward.

Power Tool 7: The Cohen Bradford model of negotiation

The Cohen Bradford model takes a six-stage approach to persuading someone based on a reciprocal approach.

Here is a summary of how to use the model.

1. Assume everyone is a potential ally
It may feel challenging to assume someone you have had difficult interactions with before – or someone you have

never met before, could be an ally. This is where you have to go to work on managing conflict and your inner diva as discussed in Chapter 6.

Starting with this assumption will actually help you to reduce barriers with 'difficult' people as well as deal with your own concerns. Use it to help you get to a win-win mind-set and focus on what could be possible in the future rather than harp on the past.

2. Clarify your goals and priorities
Think about what you want from this person, why you have chosen them and what your primary and secondary outcomes are from the conversation.

3. Diagnose the world of the other person
Consider how the person you are meeting with is 'measured' at work and what their primary responsibilities are. Think about the people around them – what is peer pressure like from their managers or colleagues? Think about the prevailing culture in their environment and what seems to be important to them.

4. Identify relevant currencies
The Cohen-Bradford model identifies five different currencies of exchange. Your job in this stage of applying the model is to identify which currencies would be of value to the person you are going to meet.

The 5 currencies are:
   i) Inspiration-related currencies such as contribution to worthwhile causes, the chance of helping someone out, their sense of integrity and value

ii) Task-related currencies resources that can be exchanged resources such as money, staff, supplies, expertise, Finance
iii) Position-related currencies where you might offer to put in a good word, chance to work/meet with someone important)
iv) Relationship-related currencies - offering them emotional support, time and understanding, listening to them and showing appreciation
v) Personal-related currencies allowing them freedom, giving them space, keeping things simple

In this step you take some time to think about what is important to the person you are about to meet, so that you can offer that when you meet them.

5. Develop a strong relationship

This step is really about taking time to get to know them. You might speak with others who have worked with them beforehand. When you are with them, listen actively to what they have to say, build their trust and talk about things that matter to them.

Express your gratitude where they offer to assist you and keep looking for ways to help them out.

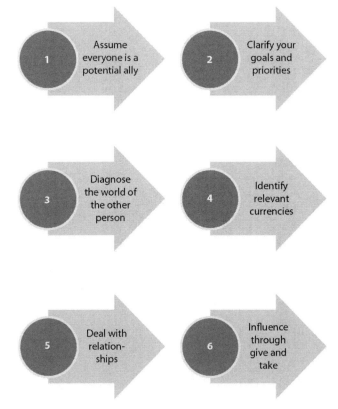

Fig 5. The Cohen Bradford Model

Addendum 2 - Some Strategies Employed by Successful Female Leaders to Overcome Underlying Challenges

Women who have succeeded in reaching high levels of seniority during their careers have shared the following strategies with me that they have previously adopted to move beyond the challenges they faced.

They are included here for your consideration as options that may support you in fulfilling on your purpose and delivering your proposition.

Please bear in mind that these strategies worked within a certain set of conditions and that you will have to evaluate how well they will work in your situation before you adopt them.

Managing profile
- Take on high profile projects and ensure excellent delivery to increase their visibility and impact
- Build relationships and increase awareness of your capacity and capability by moving sideways to positions that provide access to key stakeholders
- Understand the bigger picture and see the connections, opportunities, dependencies and risks.
- Manage and deliver across a broad portfolio by using your direct team and matrix talent with the right expertise – thereby expanding your relationships and visibility
- Prove you can hold down challenging leadership positions

Career Development
- Take on roles outside your comfort zone; use your interpersonal skills to help you learn on the job
- Move sideways or down a peg for a short time in order to maintain interest in your work
- Become a trusted advisor/sounding board on particular topics or relationships
- Have your family first and then go to university once the children are independent. Thereby making work the second chapter of your life
- Go for roles you want, not just in order to be successful, but use the learning from those efforts to lead you to greater achievements
- Make sure you get support from sponsors and leaders when applying for new roles/promotion

Confidence
- Visualise yourself as a leader
- Focus on roles that play to your strengths
- Work with managers and roles in which you gel or proactively find a better match when you don't
- Deal with your disempowering internal dialogue

Challenging Colleagues/Bullying
- Understand and read people's feelings and motives from which to build strong relation-ships
- Encourage collaborative work by caring about the achievements of each other thereby breaking down blame cultures and dysfunctional behaviour between teams
- Understand your team's strengths, weaknesses and aspirations
- Use your relationships and work with corporate processes to get decisions made and things done

- Manage conflicting priorities positively
- Actively use your emotional intelligence skills such as empathy and relating well with people

Unwritten Rules/Old Boys Club
- Find out who is in the club, what the rules are and join in
- Be more political: less effort on task delivery and more on building relationships internally
- Challenge thinking and dogma, disrupting the way things have always been done, redefine roles, challenge stereotypes and get more flexibility
- Focus on results, customers or employees instead of the politics

Family Commitments
- Increase capacity to focus on work by collaborating with partner on the balance of non-work commitments, e.g. helping a partner change their work habits by taking on more/all household duties
- Find environments with jobs, colleagues and managers who are supportive of you working part-time, compressed hours or working from home when required/possible
- Know when to say no if people at either home or work are tipping the balance that has already been negotiated and agreed to

Addendum 3 – What You Can Do for Your Organisation

The business case for diversity and increasing the female population at senior leadership levels is well understood and generally accepted.

Once you have produced results for yourself, you may want to support your organisation in empowering other female leaders.

In addition to being a great female role model and sponsoring upcoming high potentials, there are some specific initiatives that you can encourage your organisation to invest in.

For those of you who are interested, I have summarised some potential initiatives here that I have observed in my work with women and organisations.

Proven Strategies that Work for Organisations to Empower the Female Talent Pipeline

1. Ensure female talent receive regular feedback and reinforcement.
2. Women in particular appreciate regular, constructive and compassionately delivered feedback. Both positive reinforcement and ideas on how they can improve.
3. Develop leaders to invest in understanding their team members' motivations, identifying where they fit with the organisation and team strategy and coaching them to perform at their best
4. Ensure leaders and managers are educated in the organisation's policies and understand why they are relevant. Particular areas for attention as identified

by our research are bullying, flexible working and sponsorship of promotions
5. Soft audit the organisation's best practices and policies to ensure they are working as per 2. Above
6. Implement the full cultural shift across the organisation from a focus on 'hours worked' and 'time in the office' to a focus on 'value delivered'
7. Create, join and leverage industry sector based mentoring programmes such as FastForward15 (http://www.fastforward15.co.uk/)

Some Ideas for Leading the Pack

1. Understand the DNA of successful female executives in the organisation and base your recruitment and development programmes on delivering that DNA. Make sure you track how this changes over time and use it to inform strategic planning
2. Benchmark the challenges faced by women in the organisation against industry sector and best practice organisations to inform the female talent development agenda. Make sure to track how this changes over time and use it to inform strategic planning
3. Ensure development initiatives for women take a whole life approach.
4. Today's technology and ways of working mean that the distinction between work and home is blurring.
5. Learning and development programmes – particularly those focused on developing the female talent pool need to account for this
6. Use the benefits of information available from 'big data' to implement processes, policies and remuneration packages that are flexible and tailored at a higher level of granularity

7. Look at challenges and contributions of the different age groups in the workforce and conduct a cost benefit analysis to identify how to leverage the best of each generation

Even one of these initiatives, if newly implemented in your organisation can massively impact your female talent pipeline.

My website **www.authenticyoubook.com** will feature in depth articles on each of these topics over the coming year.

References:

1. *Allen, J. and Whybrow, A. (2007). Gestalt Coaching. In Palmer, S., & Whybrow, A. (Ed.), Handbook of Coaching Psychology: A Guide for Practitioners. Sussex: Routledge.*
2. *Argyris, C. (1991). Teaching smart people how to learn. Cambridge: Harvard Business Review.*
3. *Bennis, W. and Thomas, R. J. (2011). Crucibles of Leadership. In HBR's 10 must reads on leadership. Boston, Mass: Harvard Business Review Press.*
4. *Berne, E. (1961). Transactional analysis in psychotherapy. New York: Grove Press.*
5. *Berne, E. (1975). What do you say after you say hello?: the psychology of human destiny. London: Random House/Corgi.*
6. *Chaskalson, M. (2011) The Mindful Workplace: Developing Resilient Individuals and Resonant Organizations with MBSR. Wiley-Blackwell*
7. *Cohen, A.R and Bradford, D. L. (2005) Influence Without Authority. John Wiley & Sons.*
8. *Cowan, D. E. and Carey, K. (2015) Seeing Beyond Illusions: Freeing Ourselves from Ego, Guilt, and the Belief in Separation. Weiser Books.*
9. *Critchley, B. (2010). Relational coaching: Taking the coaching high road. Journal of Management Development, 29(10), 851-864.*
10. *De Haan, E. (2008). I doubt therefore I coach: practice and research. Consulting Psychology Journal, 60(1), 91-105.*
11. *De Vries, M. K. (2010). Leadership coaching and the rescuer syndrome: How to manage both sides of the*

couch. *Insead Working Paper Collections, 104(EFE/IGLC), 1-29.*

12. Ditzler, J. (2006). *Your Best Year Yet.* Harper Element.
13. Frambach, L. (2003). The weighty world of nothingness: Salomon Friedlaender's "Creative indifference". In Spagnuolo Lobb, M., & Amendt-Lyon, N. (Ed.), *Creative license: The art of gestalt therapy* (pp. 113-127). New York: Springer.
14. Fredrickson, B. L. (2009). *Positivity.* Harmony.
15. Freud, S. (1912). The Dynamics of Transference. *The Standard Edition of The Complete Works of Sigmun Freud. Volume X11.* London: Hogarth
16. Goleman, D. (1998). *Working with emotional intelligence.* New York: Bantam Books.
17. Heron, J. (1992). *Feeling and personhood - psychology in another key.* London: Sage.
18. Jahn, R and Dunne, B (2011). *Consciousness and the Source of Reality.* ICRL Press.
19. Kolb, D. A. (1984). *Experiential learning: experience as the source of learning and development.* New Jersey: Prentice Hall.
20. Korotkov, K. (2013) *Energy of Your Thoughts: How Your Thoughts Influence The World.* CreateSpace Independent Publishing Platform
21. Lapworth, P., Sills, C., & & Fish, S. (2001). The comparative script system. *Integration in counselling and psychotherapy* (pp. 117-127). London: Sage.
22. Miller, A. (2008). *The drama of being a child : The search for the true self.* London: Virago.
23. O'Neill, M. B. (2003). *Executive coaching with backbone and heart: A systems approach to engaging leaders with their challenges.* San Francisco: Jossey-Bass
24. Peters, T. (1997). The Brand Called You. *Fast Company Magazine.*

25. Rogers, C. R. (1980). *A way of being.* Boston: Houghton Miffin.
26. Shapiro, S. L. and Carlson, L. E. (2009) *The Art and Science of Mindfulness: Integrating Mindfulness into Psychology and the Helping Professions.* Americal Psychological Association.
27. Sharmer, O., & Kaufer, K. (2013). *Leading from the emerging future- from ego-system to eco-system economies.* San Francisco: Berrett-Koehler.
28. Sills, C. & Salters, D. (1991). *The comparative script system.* ITA News, Autumn
29. Smith, A. (2015). *Practical NLP 4: Submodalities And Anchoring.* Coaching Leaders.

About the Author

Ishreen Bradley is a passionate pioneer of parity in organisations. Her work is always based on a strong foundation of research.

In 2015, Ishreen published a white paper on her research with over 1000 women into the strategies women can apply to be more successful at work. This white paper is widely acknowledged as one of the most progressive and valuable contributions on the subject.

Ishreen is currently steering an initiative for WIPP International to impact gender parity through corporate and public policy.

Her contribution to empowering women has been recognised in Washington through an award from The International Alliance of Women.

With a focus on cultural transformation for parity, Ishreen works at the organisational, group and individual level to develop skills and environments that provide everyone with an equal opportunity of success through merit.

People work with Ishreen to increase their self-belief and capacity to deliver excellent results, expand their ability to lead in complex and challenging situations, then achieve and perform at progressively senior levels. Organisations engage Ishreen to evolve a culture and environment that lets the best talent shine through.

Professional Experience

Having started work as an engineer, Ishreen soon became fascinated with what causes people to be successful at work. In various roles ranging from training and quality management to sales, marketing and executive consulting – latterly in a senior position at Cap Gemini Ernst & Young, she continued to be uniquely aware of the challenges faced by non-dominants at work. As a single mother in a mobile job, she herself had to overcome some of the challenges faced in order to succeed. For the last 14 years, Ishreen has brought the benefit of her experience to thousands of leaders around the world though her consulting practice, Bizas.

Acknowledgements

My heartfelt thanks to the women and men who contributed so generously to my own growth - your loving blend of gentle guidance, ruthless compassion and wisdom is made available to the world through this book.

I would also like to express my gratitude to the many people who saw me through the creation of this book; all those who provided support, talked things over, read, wrote, offered comments, allowed me to quote their remarks and assisted with the editing, proof reading and design. Special mention goes to Mindy Gibbins-Klein for inspiring me to write, Rahima Begum for the beautiful illustrations that help bring this book to life and Julia Kingsford for moving this book from manuscript to print.

Printed in Great Britain
by Amazon